CONTENTS

Nature's
Cures

What you should know

Betsy A. Hornick, M.S., R.D.
Eric Yarnell, N.D., R.H. (A.H.G.)

Publications International, Ltd.

Nutrition Content:
Betsy A. Hornick, M.S., R.D., is a registered dietitian specializing in nutrition education and communications. She has contributed to numerous nutrition and health education publications for both consumers and health professionals, including *The Weight-Loss Bible*, *The Healthy Beef Cookbook*, and various materials published by the American Dietetic Association. She is a regular contributor to *Diabetic Cooking* magazine.

Herb Content:
Eric Yarnell, N.D., R.H. (A.H.G.) is a naturopathic physician and registered herbalist in private practice specializing in men's health and urology. He is an assistant professor in the botanical medicine department at Bastyr University in Seattle and is president of the Botanical Medicine Academy. He is the author of several textbooks including *Naturopathic Gastroenterology*, *Naturopathic Urology and Men's Health*, and *Clinical Botanical Medicine*, and he writes a regular column on herbal medicine for *Alternative and Complementary Therapies*.

Contributing Writers: Densie Webb, Ph.D., R.D.; Susan Male Smith, M.A., R.D.

Copyright © 2006 Publications International, Ltd. All rights reserved. This book may not be reproduced or quoted in whole or in part by any means whatsoever without written permission from:

Louis Weber, CEO
Publications International, Ltd.
7373 North Cicero Avenue
Lincolnwood, Illinois 60712

Permission is never granted for commercial purposes.

ISBN-13: 978-1-4127-1330-6
ISBN-10: 1-4127-1330-7

Manufactured in U.S.A.

8 7 6 5 4 3 2 1

INTRODUCTION: FOOD FOR THOUGHT—AND BETTER HEALTH

※ ※ ※

Eat to live: That's the message of this book. But we don't mean getting a grip on your appetite. Rather, we're talking about utilizing nature's bounty to preserve and protect your health.

With so much attention on America's obesity epidemic and various weight-loss diets, you could easily get the impression that food is your enemy. Carbohydrate, fat, and protein have all been vilified, sometimes simultaneously.

But these nutrients are critical to good health. They're part of Mother Nature's pharmacy. Food and herbs, if you know how to use them, can be the best preventive medicine. And they can help you cope with and even cure some unpleasant conditions and diseases.

Many of the most common ailments we face today—from annoying problems like constipation to more serious conditions such as heart disease and cancer—are linked to what we eat. Within the last several decades, research has expanded its focus to the possible links between nutrition and health; it now includes not only the potential dangers of eating certain foods (or too much of certain foods) but also the healing and protective powers that some foods and herbs possess. While they cannot take the place of medical treatment, it is increasingly evident that food and herbs have significant disease-fighting potential. That means you have the power to choose foods and herbs that may help prevent and treat a host of the most common maladies.

You've probably heard that scientists have identified specific nutrients or substances that may play a role in preventing, causing, or treating certain diseases. But we eat foods, not just nutrients. Your overall diet is more than the sum of its parts. Sub-

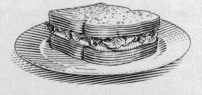

stances in foods interact in powerful ways that can have profound effects on your health. So you can't focus just on specific components of food, such as carbohydrate, protein, fat, vitamins, or minerals. If you do, you may overlook some important substances that can enhance your health.

That's where this book comes in. In Part I, we've spotlighted common health problems that appear to have a link to nutrition. Turn to this section to understand how specific diseases and conditions may be affected by diet. You'll learn which foods and herbs might be useful in their prevention or treatment. We've skipped the hype to present a balanced, evidence-based approach to using food and herbs to your health advantage. Since nutrition science is continuously evolving, we've pointed out where evidence is more—or less—definitive. We've also translated current science dealing with nutrients and other substances into practical advice.

In Part II, you'll learn how to create a varied, balanced diet that promotes good health. The major food groupings are presented, with an emphasis on the specific foods and eating patterns that are known to provide health benefits. Here you'll find tips for choosing, storing, preparing, and serving various foods to preserve and enhance their disease-fighting potential.

Part III introduces you to the healing power of herbs. While using herbs to improve health may seem exotic, they are actually the source of many of today's drugs. It's only natural that we should explore their beneficial effects, too. We've highlighted herbs that can help improve the conditions reviewed in Part I, although they have additional health benefits as well. And we've included important information about safely buying herbal products.

Mother Nature has put healing medicine in an easy-to-swallow package. *Nature's Cures* will help you put her vast disease-fighting arsenal to work for your own health's sake.

PART I

✳ ✳ ✳

PREVENTING
AND
HEALING ILLNESS

ARTHRITIS

✖ ✖ ✖

It's a common tabloid headline—"Miracle Cure for Arthritis!" Arthritis is the kind of disease that's a perfect target for such scams. It's not well understood, so anything goes when it comes to theories and treatments. And arthritis often strikes older folks, who are favorite targets of charlatans.

If you suffer from arthritis, you know how desperate you can get for relief. You may feel you have nothing to lose by trying an alleged cure. After all, your own doctor may not be able to offer much relief, and what medicines there are—primarily nonsteroidal anti-inflammatory drugs and steroids—have limited benefits and may cause some unpleasant side effects, as well.

Most important for scam artists, arthritis is unpredictable, with natural flare-ups and remissions. This, of course, makes it very difficult for patients to know for sure if any improvement is the result of a specific treatment or just a normal remission. Arthritis is a natural for the placebo effect, when the patient's *expectation* that a treatment will work can actually result in improvement.

Many Diseases, One Name

Arthritis isn't really a single disease at all. It's a term used to describe more than 100 disorders known collectively as rheumatic diseases. Although the Greek word *arthritis* literally means "joint inflammation," even this classic symptom isn't present in all types.

Take *osteoarthritis* (OA), the most common form of arthritis. It often involves no inflammation. OA is a degenerative joint disease; weight-bearing joints simply wear themselves out. This is a stereotypical condition of old age, but it's not uncommon in the younger crowd. It's particularly common among athletes (baseball players, golfers, tennis players), typists, pianists—anyone who pounds joints.

It may start, for whatever reason (maybe heredity), with the thinning out of cartilage between joints. Eventually, wear and tear destroys the cartilage.

This creates painful bone-on-bone rubbing.

If you're overweight, you're more likely to develop OA, because there's more stress and strain on your joints, particularly your knees. Research shows that, conversely, if you lose excess weight—at least 11 pounds, according to one study of overweight middle-aged women—you can cut in half your risk of developing OA of the knee.

Rheumatoid arthritis (RA) is practically a different disease altogether. It's characterized by inflamed knuckles and joints and, often, misshapen hands. People who have RA and other forms of arthritis must endure endless episodes of swollen, red, painfully stiff joints. RA, like the related disorder lupus, is an autoimmune disease, which means the body is literally attacking itself. And the battle isn't confined to the joints. The entire body is affected, sometimes causing fatigue, loss of appetite, even fever.

The desperation bred by the mystery and misery of RA could explain why, according to estimates, most sufferers have tried as many as 13 different arthritis remedies in search of relief. Diets and food cures seem to lead the pack.

Although the inventory of unfounded arthritis cures is long, there is a short list of dietary factors with healing potential. Most of the promising nutrition research has involved RA. In addition to diet, some relief from discomfort may also be found through weight loss and exercise.

Finned Ammunition

Hope has been raised most by fish oils, of all things. It's the omega-3 fatty acids in fish—the same stuff people were popping in the mid '80s to fend off heart disease—that may offer relief.

It's not such a fishy finding. Omega-3 fatty acids are known to exert anti-inflammatory action by prompting the body to decrease inflammation. Several studies of RA sufferers have reported an easing of joint pain and less fatigue after taking fish oils; the discomfort and fatigue returned when the supplements were discontinued.

But this connection is far from proven and certainly not a cure. Despite optimistic results from omega-3s, the disease

GOOD FOODS TO CHOOSE

A 3½-ounce serving of the following fish provides at least 700 milligrams (0.7 gram) of omega-3 fatty acids:

Anchovies *
Bass, striped
Bluefish
Herring *
Mackerel *
Sablefish *
Salmon
Sardines *
Shark
Trout, brook
Trout, lake *
Tuna, white

* These contain double the omega-3s, or at least 1.4 grams.

In general, the darker the flesh, the fattier the fish and the more omega-3s it contains.

remains active, the relief is modest, and it appears that the therapy may need to be continued on a long-term basis to be of any real help. Don't start popping fish-oil capsules without your health care professional's approval, either. There can be serious side effects, including prolonged bleeding and an increased risk of stroke.

Then again, it certainly can't hurt to start eating more fish; it's part of a healthful diet anyway. Some reports say a half pound of fish a day may do the trick. If you can't manage that, try two or three servings a week. (See Good Foods to Choose, at left, for fishy omega-3 sources, and see Omega-3s for Landlubbers on the next page for nonfish sources of these fatty acids.)

Roots to the Rescue

Gingerroots (technically the underground stems or rhizomes) have a long history of use in India for people with OA and RA. This spicy addition to many Asian cuisines reduces inflammation by blocking the cyclooxygenase (COX) enzyme—the very same enzyme that medications called COX-2 inhibitors, such as Celebrex, were developed to suppress. Most of the Cox-2 medications, however, were taken off the market because of cardiovascular side effects. Nonsteroidal anti-inflammatory drugs are also used to treat OA and RA, but they irritate the stomach. Ginger does not cause stomach irritation; in fact, it protects the digestive tract by increasing blood flow to the stomach, which brings with it bicarbonate to help control stomach acid. Consume at least a two-inch cube of fresh rhizome or 1 to 2 teaspoons ginger

OMEGA-3s FOR LANDLUBBERS

Beans, dried
Broccoli
Canola oil
Chinese greens
Flaxseed oil
Flaxseeds, ground
Kale
Legumes
Salad greens
Soybeans
Soy milk
Soy oil
Tofu
Walnut oil
Walnuts
Wheat germ

powder (less than six months old) two or three times per day. Larger amounts may be recommended by an herbal practitioner if your arthritis is severe.

The Allergy Angle

Because RA symptoms come and go, it's tempting to blame the condition on food allergies. (And there seems no end to the number of hucksters willing to charge RA sufferers countless dollars for bogus "antiallergy diet plans.") About a third of RA sufferers do claim that certain foods trigger flare-ups of their symptoms. The connection could just be coincidence. But if an allergic reaction can indeed provoke symptoms, it's likely to be very individual. There is no one food that can trigger arthritis symptoms in everyone. That means there is no single food everyone can avoid or one diet for all to follow that could cure this condition.

If you want to test yourself for food allergies, visit a registered dietitian so you can be monitored on a nutritionally sound elimination diet. Such a regimen starts with a simple diet that eliminates any possible allergy-producing foods, then adds them back one at a time, so that any consequences can be observed. A caution: Beware of any diet that eliminates entire food groups for a long period of time.

In any case, try to protect yourself from food-borne illnesses, as these can precipitate a temporary attack of Reiter's syndrome, a reactive arthritis triggered by eating contaminated food.

BIRTH DEFECTS

✖ ✖ ✖

The old saying goes that a pregnant woman is eating for two. The new twist on that old wisdom (this time backed by solid research) is that a woman should be eating for two *before* she becomes pregnant—certainly in terms of the quality of her diet if not truly in terms of quantity.

It's only been fairly recently that science has shown us just how much is at stake if a woman's nutritional status is not up to snuff when she conceives. Certain aspects of the fetus's normal development depend greatly on the mother's nutrition before she becomes pregnant. One of the most crucial links is that between the mother-to-

be's intake of folic acid and neural-tube birth defects in her child. If the woman is at a healthy, appropriate weight for her size when she conceives, this also appears to have a beneficial effect on pregnancy outcome.

Of course, a woman's nutrition and lifestyle *during* pregnancy can greatly affect her chances of delivering a healthy baby, too. Adequate weight gain during pregnancy is important for reducing the chance of having a low-birth-weight infant, who has a higher risk of health problems as a result. Avoiding toxic substances—such as alcohol, tobacco, marijuana, and other illegal drugs, and even many legal medications—during pregnancy also increases the likelihood of having a healthy baby.

Folic Acid and Neural-Tube Defects

By getting enough of the B vitamin folic acid in the month before she conceives and during the first several weeks of her pregnancy, a woman can help prevent a group of birth defects in her child known collectively as neural-tube defects (or NTDs). In NTDs, the central nervous system (the brain and spinal cord) and/or its coverings do not finish developing properly. Often, a portion of the brain or spinal cord is left undeveloped or dangerously exposed.

In the NTD anencephaly, the brain is severely underdeveloped.

In spina bifida, part of the spinal cord is exposed or defective. Spina bifida is currently the number-one disabling birth defect. The hope is that with the knowledge of the folic-acid connection, many future tragedies of this type can be prevented.

NTDs are the only birth defects to be so directly linked to the mother's nutritional status. But, in an ironic twist, traditional prenatal care may not prevent NTDs; often, by the time a pregnant woman visits her physician and begins taking prenatal supplements that provide folic acid, it is already too late to prevent an NTD. That's because *all* NTDs occur in the first four weeks after conception. After that, spinal-cord development is complete. Most women, however, don't even know they're pregnant until at least three weeks after conception, and many don't seek medical care for days or weeks after that. So, it's clear: Any woman who *might* become pregnant (close to half of all pregnancies are unplanned) should get plenty of folic acid through her diet and/or supplementation.

Indeed, the U.S. Public Health Service now recommends that *any* woman capable of becoming pregnant consume 0.4 milligram (400 micrograms) of folic acid a day.

Besides multivitamins or prenatal vitamins, food sources of folic acid include fortified breads, cereals, rice, pasta, and other grain foods. The Food and Drug Administration (FDA) now mandates that manufacturers add folic acid to enriched grain products (breads, flour, cereals, crackers, cornmeal, rice, pasta), just as they add other B vitamins and iron. Some breakfast cereals are fortified with the full 400 micrograms of folic acid per serving. (Check the labels on grain products to ensure the products you choose are providing you with enough folic acid every day.)

One important point to note: *Folate* is actually the naturally occurring form of this B vitamin; *folic acid* is the synthetic

GOOD SOURCES OF FOLATE

Asparagus
Avocados
Beans, dried (black,
         garbanzo, kidney,
         lima, pinto, white)
Beets
Broccoli
Brussels sprouts
Carrots
Cauliflower
Greens, cooking
         (mustard, turnip)
Greens, salad (chicory,
         endive, escarole,
         romaine)
Kale
Lentils
Liver (calf, chicken,
         pork, turkey)
Oranges, orange juice
Parsnips
Peanuts
Peas, dried and green
Spinach
Tomato juice
Wheat germ

form found in supplements and fortified foods. Folic acid is more easily absorbed by the body. Folic acid is also the form of the vitamin that studies have linked to decreased risk of NTDs. On the other hand, since your body requires this B vitamin (in either form) for proper protein metabolism, for cell division, and to make the red blood cells that carry life-giving oxygen throughout your body, it's still important for men, women, and children who do not take vitamin supplements to get plenty of naturally occurring folate from their diet. Good food sources of folate include leafy green vegetables (such as romaine and endive lettuce and mustard greens), broccoli, legumes (dried beans and peas and lentils), and orange juice.

CANCER

�֎ ✖ ✖

Cancer. The word itself is enough to make you shudder. Perhaps one of the most frightening aspects of the disease is that there is still so much we don't know about it. But progress is being made in understanding the contributing factors and in developing treatments. Heredity influences your risk of developing certain cancers, but factors considered "environmental"—such as smoking and alcohol consumption—appear to play important roles, too. Another environmental influence that has garnered more and more attention is diet—both in terms of its role in triggering cancer and its potential role in helping to prevent it. Indeed, according to the American Institute for Cancer Research (AICR), 30 to 40 percent of all cancers are directly linked to food, physical activity, and body weight. Unlike heredity, diet is one of the possible cancer contributors that we can change (along with smoking and drinking habits).

So what dietary choices can you make to help lessen your risk? *That's* the catch. We don't know all the answers yet, but we suspect we're close to quite a few. And some of those suspicions may be worth acting on now.

The Big Picture

Cancer, the number two killer in the United States, isn't a single disease. Cancer is an umbrella term for more than 200 different conditions, which all have in common the out-of-control growth of cells. Each type of cancer is unique, with its own set of triggers and treatments. Proving a dietary link to cancer is not easy. Although the connection to some types of cancer seems more solid, some suspected ties are merely educated guesses based on statistics from epidemiology. Epidemiology is a branch of science that observes and compares the rates of diseases in different environments and situations. Actual clinical trials that put theories to the ultimate test are expensive and difficult to design, and they cannot provide valid results for decades, because cancer takes that long to develop.

For years, scientists focused on specific substances in foods that might *cause* cancer. At first, suspicions centered around manmade creations, such as additives, artificial sweeteners, and pesticides. Then researchers refocused their attention on the many *natural* toxins in foods that were potentially cancerous, such as aflatoxins in peanuts and solanine in potatoes.

Today, the dietary fight against cancer has progressed further still. These days, when we talk about taking dietary steps to prevent cancer, we're talking about being proactive. Today's preventive strategies go beyond simply avoiding potentially cancer-causing substances in certain foods to actually using diet to strengthen the body's defenses against cancer and toxic substances. Indeed, there's more and more evidence that what you *do* eat can actually offer protection against, and therefore lower your chances of developing, cancer. Food has gone from enemy to ally. What's more, a diet that may help protect against cancer appears remarkably similar to a diet that is heart healthy and weight wise as well.

ANTIOXIDANTS TO THE RESCUE

Much of the cancer-protective promise of certain foods appears to stem from antioxidant nutrients concentrated in those foods. An antioxidant is a substance that protects the body's cells from oxidation, the chemical process in which oxygen molecules attach to almost anything in their path, creating destructive compounds called free radicals. Free radicals aren't foreign invaders. They are normal inhabitants of your body, produced in response to everyday chemical reactions that normally occur in your body.

Your body has a built-in protection mechanism and can, to some extent, guard itself against the damaging chain reactions that free radicals set off. But sometimes free radicals get out of control, outpacing the body's natural repair system, such as when too many are produced in response to cigarette smoke, ultraviolet light, and environmental pollutants including smog, car exhaust, and ozone. Left unchecked, they run amok, causing damage and altering the genetic makeup of the normal cells in your body. This type of genetic alteration can pave the way for cancer.

You can see evidence of simple oxidation when a car rusts, when butter turns rancid, and when a cut apple turns brown. But dip an apple in lemon juice immediately after you cut it and—voilà!—it remains white. Why? The vitamin C in the lemon juice is an antioxidant, and it protects the apple from oxidation. In essence, the same thing happens in your body, on a grander scale. Free radicals are thought to cause damage that may lead not only to cancer but to other conditions that become more common with age (and therefore with greater free-radical exposure), such as heart disease and cataracts. So there is hope that antioxidants from the diet can help protect against that damage and help prevent or at least delay such conditions by neutralizing free radicals.

Only certain vitamins and minerals have antioxidant properties. Three vitamins have received the most attention: vitamin A (in its beta-carotene form), vitamin C, and vitamin E. The trace mineral selenium also plays a role in the antioxidant drama, not as an antioxidant itself but as an element of an antioxidant. Riboflavin, which is one of the B vitamins, and magnesium have also been recognized as having some antioxidant properties.

FOOD TASTES BETTER, ANYWAY

While scientists often seek to identify the precise nutrients and substances that might be responsible for preventing or promot-

BOOSTING IMMUNITY

The mushroom known as turkey tail (because of its peculiar shape), *Coriolus veriscolor* or *Trames veriscolor*, has a long history of use as a food and medicine in Asia. In the last 30 years, clincial studies have shown that turkey tail strengthens the immune system, enhances conventional treatment, and increases longevity in people with cancer. Turkey tail supplements in the amount of 2 to 3 grams per day have been studied in thousands of cancer patients. Several clinical trials compared people with cancer who took turkey tail supplements and had been treated with surgery, chemotherapy, and/or radiation therapy with those who had the same treatments but did not take the supplements. Those who took the mushroom were twice as likely to still be alive three and five years after diagnosis as those who did not take turkey tail. Tests also showed that the immune function of people who took turkey tail along with chemotherapy and radiation therapy was far better than those who did not. It has not been shown to cause any side effects. For more information, see page 200.

ing cancer, we eat foods, not just nutrients. For this reason, groups such as the National Cancer Institute and AICR provide guidelines for an overall healthy, cancer-protective diet. It is most realistic and practi- cal—not to mention more enjoyable and economi- cal—to focus on eating more of the foods that contain potentially benefi- cial substances, namely fruits, vegetables, and whole grains, than on downing individual nutrients or chemicals. Besides, much of the earliest evidence suggesting foods might help protect against cancer came from observing the typical diets of select populations in which the incidence of certain cancers was much lower than in the general population. Attempts to tease out specific nutrients that might be responsible for the protection have not been successful. When the benefits are linked to a diet made up of whole foods, it is often difficult to say for certain that the protective effects were caused by one specific nutrient rather than by the interplay of all the potentially helpful substances (sometimes called phytochemicals) that are found naturally in fruits, vegetables, and whole grains. The recommendations, therefore, encourage the consumption of the whole foods rather than the single nutrients so that people don't miss out on these other potentially beneficial substances (some of which scientists may not even have identified yet).

What follows is an overview of what we know so far, what we suspect, and what we don't know about some of the foods and nutrients that may help protect against cancer and those that may promote cancer. With this knowledge, you can create a diverse diet that includes more foods that may help to protect you and your family.

Potential Cancer Fighters

To help stack your deck against cancer, consider stocking your diet with more of the foods listed in this section. Don't just add them to what you're already eating, though, unless you're trying to gain weight. Cut back on fatty foods, sugary foods that don't provide many nutrients, and other foods discussed later in the Cancer Promoters section; replace them with more foods filled with the potential cancer fighters discussed here.

BETA-CAROTENE: GOOD AND BAD NEWS

For a short time, beta-carotene, a form of vitamin A, was a star among supplements. There was good reason, too—solid research suggested that beta-carotene could lower cancer risk. Vitamin manufacturers jumped on the bandwagon and began replacing all the vitamin A in their pills with beta-carotene, until results from a study called CARET (Beta-Carotene and Retinol Efficacy Trial) brought things to a screeching halt. This landmark study, published in 1996, tested synthetic beta-carotene and vitamin A supplements in people at high risk for lung can-

BEST FOR BETA-CAROTENE

Apricots, fresh or dried; apricot nectar
Broccoli
Cantaloupe
Carrots, carrot juice
Grapefruit, red or pink
Greens, collard or mustard
Kale
Mango
Peppers, sweet red
Persimmon
Pumpkin
Spinach
Squash, winter
Sweet potato
Swiss chard

cer—smokers, former smokers, and asbestos-industry workers. The study was quickly discontinued when it became clear that those taking beta-carotene supplements (about 30 milligrams a day) actually had a higher rate of lung cancer and higher mortality rate than those taking a placebo (an inert pill).

Nevertheless, beta-carotene's action as an antioxidant can significantly slow or prevent oxidative damage in the body that can increase the risk of certain types of cancer, including oral cancers and tumors of the stomach, breast, cervix, uterus, prostate, and colon. Because vitamin A can be toxic in large doses, the emphasis is on getting it from fruits and vegetables, where it is primarily found in the form of beta-carotene, and not from supplements of vitamin A. Other carotenoids, especially lutein and lycopene, may be protective, too, but they have not been studied as well, and information on their content in foods is somewhat limited.

VITAMIN C VINDICATED

Researchers are still arguing over vitamin C and colds. But vitamin C may offer protection against lots of other conditions, including cancer. A diet high in vitamin C has been strongly linked to a lower risk of cancers of the mouth, throat, stomach, and pancreas. Weaker data exist for cancers of the breast, cervix, and rectum. However, it's hard to separate the effects of vitamin C from those of beta-carotene, because many fruits and vegetables

BEYOND CITRUS FOR C

Broccoli
Brussels sprouts
Cabbage
Cantaloupe
Cauliflower
Greens, cooking (collard,
        mustard, or turnip)
Kale
Kiwifruit
Mango
Papaya
Peppers, sweet, green or red
Potato, white or sweet
Strawberries
Tomato, tomato juice

OPTIMISM OVER E

Research appears to support vitamin E's contribution to cutting the risk of some types of cancers. The evidence is strongest for prostate cancer, where vitamin E, along with selenium, seems to offer protection. Other links include a possible reduction in the risk of cancers of the stomach and lung and perhaps of the bladder, colon, and rectum.

But vitamin E is unique. While its merit as an antioxidant is accepted by many scientists, it only appears to be of value when consumed in amounts far greater than what you can get from foods. Because vitamin E is fat soluble, the foods richest in it tend to be high in fat—such as veg-

are rich in both. In fact, studies show it may be the combination of the two that's important, which is yet another reason to get your antioxidants from foods rather than supplements whenever possible. Indeed, the few studies in which vitamin C was provided by supplement have not shown any cancer-fighting benefits.

etable oils, sunflower seeds, nuts, and wheat germ—so it's not a very practical nutrient to seek out in large amounts in the diet. Otherwise, you may find yourself overloading on calories.

What to do? As a start, be sure to eat lots of whole grains, fortified cereals, leafy greens, and fish to obtain a baseline level of E. To boost your intake into the potentially cancer-fighting range—about 100 International Units (IU) daily—without overdosing on fat, however, you would need to add a supplement. (Many studies are conducted using 800 IU, but there's evidence to show you don't need this much to gain benefits.) Although many experts are optimistic about vitamin E's possibilities, they have stopped short of recommending such a supplement until further research is done. Certainly, at this point, if you are considering a vitamin E supplement, discuss it with your health care professional first.

SELENIUM'S TIGHTROPE ACT

This mineral is not actually an antioxidant. Rather, it is part of the enzyme glutathione peroxidase, which is part of the body's antioxidant defense system, helping protect it against free radicals. You don't hear as much about selenium, however, because we still don't know that much about it. Preliminary evidence suggests a link between selenium and a reduced risk for cancers of the lung, colon, and prostate.

Getting the right amount is a balancing act that Mother Nature handles fairly well. Selenium is widely available in such foods as grains, lean meat, poultry, and fish. There is a narrow margin, however, between safe and toxic amounts of selenium. So high-dose supplements are a distinctly bad idea.

THE CALCIUM CONNECTION

The evidence supporting this newcomer to the cancer-prevention scene is a bit less conclusive yet still promising. The research suggests calcium plays a role in reducing the risk for colorectal cancer, perhaps by thwarting the ability of cancerous cells to gain a foothold in the lining of the intestines or by binding with them, rendering them benign. Calcium-rich foods seem to offer more protection than calcium supplements.

Many Americans fall short of the recommended daily intake for calcium, which is 1,300 milligrams for teenagers; 1,000 milligrams for adults 19 to 50 years of age; and 1,200 milligrams for adults 51 years of age and older. Amounts of 1,200 to 1,500 milligrams have been linked to an anticancer effect. On the other hand, there is evidence that an intake of more than 2,000 milligrams of calcium  per day, primarily from supplements, may increase the risk for prostate cancer.

In light of this, both men and women are best off meeting recommended levels of calcium primarily from food sources (since it's far more difficult to overdose on a vitamin or mineral when you get it from food than when you take supplements). Calcium sources include milk, yogurt, cheese, fortified juice, sardines with bones, salmon, and some leafy green vegetables (bok choy, broccoli, kale, and turnip and collard greens). If you obtain much of your calcium from dairy products, select low-fat or nonfat varieties to help keep your intake of total and saturated fat low. If you take a calcium supplement, consult with a registered dietitian or your doctor to determine how much is appropriate for you to take.

FIBER FALLOUT

The research on fiber in the prevention of colon cancer is positive, even if the link is somewhat shaky. There are a variety of ways that fiber may protect: by diluting toxins, by altering conditions within the bowel, and by literally getting carcinogens out faster. The numerous variables are what confuse the issue. In fact, as more knowledge of fiber's potential actions has accrued, the link has become *less* clear.

This may be partly due to the failure of many past studies to separate out the effects of *soluble* versus *insoluble* fibers. It's the insoluble type—as in wheat bran—that probably provides the most protection. But other studies have also found a protective effect from fruits and vegetables, which are higher in soluble fiber. To confuse matters further, several large studies even found that overall fiber intake does not seem to have any significant effect on lowering colon-cancer risk. Fiber's effect also may depend on whether your diet is high in fat, too.

But don't mistake the forest for the trees. Because fiber is clearly beneficial to many other conditions, it's wise to make sure you are consuming adequate amounts. Furthermore, foods high in fiber are also known to contain other healthful substances that *do* have protective effects against cancer.

Experts advise aiming for 20 to 35 total grams of fiber each day. Most Americans, however, eat less than half this amount. If your diet is low in fiber, try gradually substituting foods made with whole grains for those made with refined grains, and work up to eating at least five servings of fruits and vegetables a day.

FOODS WITH EMERGING PROMISE

Compelling evidence is accumulating for the anticancer properties of more foods and food components. For example, the antioxidants in tea, called catechins, may inhibit the growth of cancerous cells. Green tea contains more of these antioxidants than black tea, possibly because it is subject to less processing. One catch: To release about 80 percent of its catechins, you must steep your tea for about five minutes.

Red wine is rich in phytochemicals, particularly compounds called polyphenols, which include catechins and resveratrol. These anticancer antioxidant compounds are found in the skin and seeds of grapes. And garlic contains organic allyl sulfur compounds that seem to help slow or prevent the growth of tumor cells.

Cancer Promoters

While you're opting for more foods with cancer-fighting properties, you should also keep tabs on your intake of certain foods and other aspects of your overall diet that may actually aid cancer's growth or development and do your best to limit these. Adding potentially helpful foods and losing possible dietary dangers can equal a more cancer-protective diet all around.

FAT IS WHERE IT'S AT

Fat has been found guilty of contributing to the development of a number of diseases, and cancer is no exception. High-fat diets have been linked to an increase in the risk of cancers of the colon, rectum, prostate, and endometrium. At one time, the breast-cancer link was just as strong; however, the prestigious Nurses' Health Study at Harvard refuted this link when researchers found no difference in cancer risk between those eating 50 percent of their calories from fat and those consuming less than 30 percent.

Scientists are unclear, however, about how high-fat diets are involved in cancer risk. It may be the total amount of fat, the type of fat, the calories contributed by fat, some other factor associated with high-fat foods, or a combination of these factors. For example, fats such as the saturated fat in meats, the omega-3 fats in fish, and the monounsaturated fats in olive oil likely differ in their effects on cancer risk. Cooking methods used for higher-fat foods, such as meats, may be a factor. In addition, high-fat diets tend to be high in calories, which often leads to unwanted weight gain. Overweight and obese individuals are at higher risk for developing several types of cancer.

Even if fat *does* affect cancer risk, it's not as a *cause* but rather as a *promoter* of the disease. That means it enhances the action of true carcinogens, such as tobacco smoke. Experts generally echo the advice given to prevent other chronic diseases—limit fat intake to less than 30 percent of calories. Consistent with guidelines for lowering heart-disease risk, you are wise to substitute monounsaturated fats, such as olive oil and canola oil, for some of the saturated fats in your diet (check food labels), choose smaller portions of meats, and eat more plant-based foods.

THE CALORIE CONUNDRUM

It may sound a bit absurd to say calories can cause cancer. After all, you can't stop eating. But research does suggest that an excess of calories is cancer-promoting, while being slightly underweight affords protection. This may even be a crucial part of the fat connection, considering that a gram of fat is higher in calories than a gram of carbohydrate or protein.

Being overweight is associated with higher rates of several types of cancer, including cancers of the breast (among post-menopausal women), colon, endometrium, esophagus, gallbladder, pancreas, and kidney. The best way to achieve a healthy weight is to balance energy taken in (from food calories) with energy expended (through physical activity). In fact, there is strong evidence that getting regular physical activity may reduce the risk of breast and colon cancers, and perhaps other types, as well. Adults should get at least 30 minutes of moderate activity five or more days each week; 45 minutes or more of moderate-to-vigorous activity five or more days per week may further reduce breast- and colon-cancer risk.

ALCOHOL ADVICE

There's no doubt that alcohol contributes to esophageal and oral-cavity cancers. Add cigarette smoke, and the risk skyrockets. But is there danger only for alcoholics, or should social drinkers also abstain? There have been conflicting data on moderate drinking and breast-cancer risk. It's probably best to follow the advice given for other chronic diseases: If you drink, do so only in moderation.

NITRITE/NITRATE ALERT

There seems to be a connection between processed, smoked, and salt-cured meats and cancer. One reason is the nitrites—they are added to many luncheon meats, bacon, ham, and hot dogs to maintain color and to prevent contamination with bacteria. The problem is that nitrites can be converted to carcinogenic nitrosamines in your body. Some studies have linked high intakes of processed meats with colorectal and stomach cancers.

To help counteract this effect, eat these foods along with vitamin-C-containing foods, which can help retard the conversion of nitrites into nitrosamines (the vitamin C must be in the stomach at the same time as the nitrites). Still, it may be good to go easy on processed meats. Meats preserved by smoking or salting also increase your exposure to potentially carcinogenic substances (see Unwelcome Mutagens below), so it's wise to limit these, too.

Some vegetables naturally contain nitrates, substances similar to nitrites. The use of certain fertilizers may increase the amount of nitrates in them, as well. However, many vegetables also come loaded with the built-in protection of vitamin C.

Unfortunately, that's not true for your local water supply, where nitrate contamination from fertilizers can also be a problem. Check with your local water or health department to find out about the nitrate level. If it's high, you might want to look into bottled water.

UNWELCOME MUTAGENS

Mutagens are substances that can set off sudden

changes in a cell's genetic makeup, creating potentially cancerous compounds. Whenever you brown food, mutagens may form. The more well-done your meat is, the more mutagens you are likely to consume. Because these mutagens don't form until meat is at 300 degrees Fahrenheit for a significant time, rare or medium-rare meat is not affected. Any high-temperature cooking method, such as grilling, broiling, and pan-frying, used for meat, poultry, and fish can cause a type of carcinogen called heterocyclic amines (HCAs) to form. Grilling can also carry other risks. Another carcinogen, polycyclic aromatic hydrocarbons (PAHs), can form when the fat from meats drips onto the coals, tiles, or rocks. The rising smoke and flames can leave PAHs on the surface of the meat.

On the other hand, you must be sure to cook meat well enough to kill microorganisms that can cause potentially deadly food poisoning. So what should you do? Occasional high-heat cooking is no cause for concern. Microwaving, boiling, and baking use lower cooking temperatures, so use these methods more often than the higher-temperature methods. When you cook with higher temperatures, use a meat thermometer. This way, you can gauge when meat is cooked sufficiently on the inside to kill microorganisms and then remove it immediately from the heat to avoid the formation of excess mutagens.

CATARACTS AND MACULAR DEGENERATION

✖ ✖ ✖

Cartoon characters see spots or stars before their eyes, and everyone laughs. But there's nothing funny about sight-robbing cataracts and age-related macular degeneration (AMD). Both of these eye diseases are hallmarks of aging, but that doesn't mean you must surrender your sight to them as you get on in years. Adding vision-valuable foods to your diet may help you protect your eyes from the damage that occurs over time.

Understanding Cataracts

The reality is sobering. If you live long enough, chances are you'll get cataracts. As the population ages, the numbers creep ever upward—each year, more than a million people are diagnosed with cataracts severe enough to require surgery. Almost two-thirds of all 60-year-olds have them.

A cataract starts off as a cloudy spot on the clear lens of your eye (which is located behind your colored iris), almost as if you smeared grease on it. Some cataracts develop so slowly, you aren't even aware of them. If the cataract is near the edge of the lens, it may not interfere with your vision. But often, the cataract gets worse, or you get more of them. You may begin to notice double or blurred vision, sensitivity to light (glare may be especially troublesome), and changes in color perception. The upshot will be progressively more-frequent changes in your eyeglass prescription, until the glasses no longer seem to help the problem. Your eye doctor will probably detect your cataract and, if it gets severe enough, suggest the latest in eye surgery.

Until the late 1970s, cataract surgery was certainly no picnic. It never really restored normal vision, and you had to wear thick eyeglasses, declaring to the world your advancing age. Now, cataract surgery is a mere hour-long affair, usually performed on an out-patient basis. The cloudy natural lens is removed and replaced with a plastic intraocular lens. In the vast majority of cases, the operation is extremely successful: The implanted lens restores sight lost to the clouded-over lens and corrects most of the need for eyeglasses after surgery, although glasses may still be needed in some cases for reading or distance vision.

But wouldn't preventing cataracts in the first place be even better? Well, tell those eye surgeons to hold their scalpels and lasers, because cataracts may not be the inevitable consequence of aging we've come to expect.

Making Sense of Macular Degeneration

Cataracts may affect more people, but macular degeneration is the most common cause of age-related blindness. That's why researchers are furiously working to better understand how to prevent and treat this eye disease, as well.

The macula is an area of the retina, which is in the back of your eye. The retina is like the screen onto which the lens focuses the light (and hence the images) that enters the eye. But only a small area of the retina, the macula, contains the specialized cells responsible for the sharp central vision that you need to read, drive, and perform many other daily activities requiring clear, crisp focus. As the macula degenerates, some of the messages from your eye to your brain that tell you what you're seeing can't be transmitted, and your vision slowly becomes blurred or distorted; you may see shapes, but not fine lines, and you may experience a blank spot in your central vision. Eventually, you lose your vision altogether. There is currently no effective treatment to restore vision once the macula begins to degenerate.

Researchers have discovered that the retina of the eye is constantly bathed in vitamin C, at levels much higher than those normally found in the blood. Some researchers speculate that the vitamin C is there for protection and that the amount may need bolstering as we age. Perhaps antioxidant nutrients, therefore, could help prevent this condition, too.

Visionary Nutrients

Where there's exposure to ultraviolet (UV) light (such as from the sun), there's potential for cell damage. The eye is certainly no exception. In fact, the more UV exposure, the more cataracts—up to three times the risk.

The eye is constantly exposed to light and air—typically polluted air as well—and that's just the recipe for oxidative damage (see the discussion of oxidation and antioxidants, pages 21–22, in Cancer). When cells are oxidized, they set off chain reactions that can destroy whatever is in their path—including healthy cells in the lens or the macula of the eye.

Suddenly, a dietary connection to eye disease no longer seems so far-fetched. Research into the

HOW TO SAVE YOUR SIGHT

• Limit your sun exposure between the hours of 10 A.M. and 4 P.M., when sunlight is most intense.

• Wear a wide-brimmed hat when in the sun.

• Choose sunglasses with UVA and UVB protection (they are labeled voluntarily by the manufacturer), and *wear them*.

• Stop smoking. Smoking increases the amount of oxidative damage inflicted on your eyes.

• If you have diabetes, keep your blood glucose under control. High blood glucose levels can damage the lens of the eye.

• Eat a diet rich in fruits and vegetables. Aim for five to nine servings per day. Be sure to include those rich in vitamin C and beta-carotene.

• See an eye doctor regularly for early detection.

possible connections between nutrition and vision has grown by leaps and bounds over the past decade. It is now evident that antioxidants may work to slow the progression of cataracts and may even help prevent them. The antioxidant nutrients linked to decreased cataract incidence include beta-carotene, vitamin C, and vitamin E.

In one study, women who ate lots of fruits and vegetables had a whopping 39 percent lower risk of developing severe cataracts (the kind that require surgery) than those who didn't eat much produce. Among the strongest protectors were spinach, sweet potatoes, and winter squash, all high in beta-carotene. Another study found daily intake of 180 milligrams of vitamin C from foods (nearly three times the recommended daily amount) reduced the odds of developing cataracts by nearly 50 percent.

With macular degeneration, National Eye Institute researchers were thrilled with the remarkable results from a six-year study. At least 25 percent of the people at risk for developing advanced macular degeneration experienced a protective effect from supplements containing vitamins C and E, beta-carotene, and zinc. The nutrients certainly don't cure the disease, nor will they restore vision already lost. However, they may help to slow progression of macular degeneration, a wonderful prospect for people suffering from this vision-robbing disease.

Another interesting finding from recent

FEAST FOR YOUR EYES

For vitamin C:
Broccoli*
Brussels sprouts*
Cantaloupe
Cauliflower
Citrus fruits and juices
Papaya
Strawberries
Tomato juice

For vitamin E:
Almonds
Corn and safflower oils
Eggs
Peanuts
Sunflower seeds

For beta-carotene:
Apricots
Cantaloupe
Carrots*
Leafy, dark greens*
     (kale, spinach,
       turnip and collard
       greens)
Mangoes
Peppers, red bell
Potatoes, sweet
Squash, winter

* These also supply lutein and zeaxanthin.

research is that people with higher macular concentrations of two beta-carotene cousins, called lutein and zeaxanthin, seem to experience greater protection from damage caused by sunlight and other environmental factors. Lutein and zeaxanthin are found in yellow-colored vegetables (see Feast for Your Eyes, at left). Research also suggests higher intakes of omega-3 fatty acids, which are found in higher-fat fish, soybeans, wheat germ, and canola oil, may help protect the eyes from AMD.

Admittedly, we are still in the infancy of learning about the connection between nutrition and eye disease. And not all the results from the research have been promising. But the possibilities are indeed worth looking into.

CELIAC DISEASE

For centuries, wheat has been known as the "staff of life." But this wholesome, nutritious grain can be devastating for people with a condition called celiac disease. Having this disease means that "comfort foods," like pasta and bread, and traditional holiday fare, like stuffing and fresh-baked pies and cookies, are off-limits. The reason? A protein called gluten, found in wheat, rye, barley, and oats.

How Common Is It?

The condition, also known as celiac sprue or gluten-sensitive enteropathy, is a genetic disease that runs in families, especially those of northwestern European descent. In countries such as Italy and Ireland, celiac disease is the most common genetic disease. Although it was once thought to be fairly rare in the United States, experts now believe that celiac disease is prevalent here as well, especially because many Americans have European roots. Indeed, nearly 1 in 133 Americans has celiac disease, according to a recent study by the University of Maryland Center for Celiac Research in Baltimore. Having a relative with the disease increases your risk.

Signs of Celiac

In people with celiac disease, gluten sets off an autoimmune reaction in which the body's own immune system produces antibodies that attack the small intestine, causing damage and illness. This damage impairs the small intestine's ability to absorb nutrients. Over time, this can lead to other illnesses, including delayed growth in children, malnutrition, premature osteoporosis (thinning of the bones), and cancer of the colon. Untreated celiac disease in pregnancy raises the risk of miscarriage and birth defects. Celiac disease also appears linked to a risk of other autoimmune disorders, such as type 1 diabetes and some types of arthritis.

Outward signs of this disease vary widely. Symptoms range from abdominal bloating and pain, chronic diarrhea, and weight loss to muscle cramps, joint pain, numb-

ness, or a painful skin rash. Some people experience behavior changes, such as irritability or depression, or overall fatigue.

For some people with the disease, no symptoms are evident until the disease is triggered by the stress of surgery, pregnancy, or a viral infection. In children, chronic irritability is a red flag. Other signs include failure to thrive in infants, short stature, tooth discoloration, and behavioral or learning problems.

Screening and Diagnosis

For many sufferers, it's not uncommon to be diagnosed with an assortment of ailments—such as anemia, depression, chronic fatigue, and irritable bowel syndrome—before celiac disease is fingered. This may explain why the time between the first appearance of symptoms and diagnosis can often be months or years.

Screening is quite simple: It involves a blood test that detects antibodies to gluten. Anyone with a family history of celiac disease should ask for the blood test. The "gold standard" for diagnosis is a biopsy of the small intestine. Using an endoscope (a thin, lighted tube) threaded through the mouth and down the esophagus, the doctor removes a tiny sample from the lining of the small intestine to check for damage that signals celiac disease.

If the diagnosis is confirmed, the irritating gluten protein must be completely removed from the diet for the remainder of the patient's life. In most cases, this relieves symptoms almost immediately and allows the small intestine to heal, a process that begins within days but can take up to six months.

The Gluten-Free Diet

There are no drugs to treat celiac disease, and there is no cure. The only treatment is lifetime avoidance of gluten. This means no breads, baked products, pastas, or cereals made with wheat (including spelt, triticale, and kamut), rye, barley, or oats (although there is currently some controversy over oats, which will be discussed shortly). But the list doesn't stop there. Many ingredients in processed foods are derived from the off-limit grains, including thickeners, fillers, and stabilizers in foods such as canned soups, luncheon meats, salad dressings, ice cream, pudding, pie, chewing gum, beer, canned tuna, and hot dogs, to name just a few. (See Beware Gluten on page 48 for more on what to avoid.) Even medications and mouthwash may contain gluten.

If you have celiac disease, the following are important safety steps to help you avoid gluten:

• Know the many ingredients that may harbor the forbidden gluten.

• Check the label of every food very carefully.

• Contact food and medication manufacturers if ingredients are unclear or there is any question.

• Get guidance from a doctor or dietitian experienced in working with people who have celiac disease.

• Learn from others who suffer from the disease.

• Avoid a food if there is any doubt about its ingredients, because every exposure to even a small amount of gluten causes intestinal damage.

What foods are "safe" for people with celiac disease? Fresh meats, fish, and poultry; milk, eggs, and unprocessed cheeses; dried beans; and plain, fresh or frozen fruits and vegetables are all safe to eat.

As for grains, corn and rice are the most readily available safe grains. Pure oats may also fall into this category. There are studies under way to test whether oats are safe for celiac sufferers, but the jury is definitely still out on them. Oats contain less gluten than wheat, and some people with celiac disease report that they can tolerate at least small amounts of oats without experiencing symptoms. But pure oats are very difficult to find, and oats can easily become contaminated with wheat or other gluten-containing ingredients during processing. So the prudent advice for now is to avoid oats.

Many people with celiac disease rely on homemade products that use wheat-flour substitutes, such as rice, tapioca, potato, or soy flours. In addition, specialty food companies offer gluten-free breads, pastas, and other grain-based products. (See Get Help Going Gluten-Free, above). What's more, with increased awareness and diagnosis of the disease, more gluten-free products are finding their way onto grocery-store shelves.

While the gluten-free diet may sound daunting at first, checking labels quickly becomes second nature, and it's not a bad way to see what other effects—in terms of calories, fat, vitamins, and other nutrients—a food may have on health. And for most people with celiac disease, their relief in finding a solution to their symptoms, and their ability to fend off the complica- tions of untreated celiac disease, make the diet seem a small price to pay.

BEWARE GLUTEN

The following ingredients signal a food contains gluten:

Barley	Graham
Beer	Kamut
Bread crumbs	Matzoh, matzoh meal
Bulgur	Oats
Cereal extract	Rye
Couscous	Seitan
Cracker meal	Semolina
Durum	Spelt
Farina	Triticale
Flour (unless derived from a safe grain)	Wheat (including bran, germ, starch)

These ingredients *may* contain gluten:*

Brown rice syrup

Caramel color

Dextrin (if it is wheat derived)

Flour and cereal products

Hydrolyzed vegetable or plant protein (HVP or HPP)

Malt, malt flavoring, malt vinegar

Modified food starch

Soy sauce

Textured vegetable protein (TVP)

*These ingredients should not be eaten unless you can verify that they are not derived from grains known to contain gluten.

CONSTIPATION

✖ ✖ ✖

It's tempting to chuckle at some of the commercials for laxatives that promise regularity. But if you've ever experienced the bloating, straining, pressure, and discomfort of constipation, you know it's not funny when it's happening to *you*.

Most doctors define constipation as unusually infrequent and difficult bowel movements. Many factors come together to cause this often misunderstood and often incorrectly treated condition.

What's Normal?

There actually is no "normal" number of bowel movements that everyone should have. What's *normal* for you may be quite *abnormal* for someone else. In fact, "normal" can be anywhere from three times a day to three times a week. But, generally, if you go three consecutive days without a bowel movement, your stools tend to dry out and harden in your intestinal tract, making them difficult to pass.

Misunderstanding the wide range that is considered normal is probably the most frequent reason for laxative abuse. Overuse of laxatives leads to dependence, increasing dosages, and ultimately, failure of the intestine to function properly on its own.

Constipation Causes

Common contributors to constipation include a diet

low in fiber, inadequate fluid intake, lack of exercise, and overuse of laxatives. Moreover, drugs such as antidepressants, antacids, antihistamines, diuretics, tranquilizers, iron supplements, anticonvulsants (for seizures), and antiParkinson's drugs can cause constipation or make it worse.

During pregnancy, constipation is a common side effect caused by changes in hormones and unfamiliar pressure on the bowel from the developing fetus. In older people, a poor diet may be made worse by decreased interest in food, slower metabolism, and difficulties in chewing due to dentures. In most cases, a higher-fiber diet, increased fluid intake, and exercise are your best tools for both preventing and treating constipation.

When to Be Concerned

Constipation can be extremely uncomfortable, even though it's often harmless. However, it can also signal a more serious underlying problem. Constipation that does not respond to an increase in fiber may signal potential problems that range from colon polyps to a malignancy and should be reported to your doctor. Likewise, if you notice spots of blood or have to strain uncomfortably with each bowel movement and you go less than two times per week, see your doctor. Other possible causes of chronic constipation may include a habit of ignoring the urge to defecate, hemorrhoids, lupus, Parkinson's disease, stroke, and neurological or muscular diseases, such as multiple sclerosis.

Getting "Unplugged"

To conquer constipation, increase your fiber and fluid intake. Start slowly—too much fiber too fast can cause gas, cramps, and bloating. Trial and error will help you determine what works best for you. Just as regularity varies from person to person, so does the recipe for relief.

• Gradually add high-fiber foods, until you're getting 20 to 35 grams of fiber a day (see Good Fiber Finds on page 52).

• Drink plenty of fluids—at least six to eight cups a day.

• Exercise regularly (at least 30 minutes a day, 5 times a week, even if it's just walking).

• Don't ignore the urge to defecate.

• Eat more prunes and figs and drink more prune juice. They contain the natural laxative isatin.

• Try a cup of coffee. The bitter-tasting constituents in coffee, and all bitter-tasting foods, stimulate the digestive tract. If you don't like coffee, try an herb called Oregon grape. The root of this plant and some close cousins such as barberry have been used safely since ancient times to overcome occasional constipation. Mix ½ teaspoon Oregon grape tincture in water and sip slowly before eating for best results.

• Use a fiber supplement. These over-the-counter products, sometimes called stool softeners, absorb water in the intestine to soften and bulk up stools, making them easier to pass. Examples include: psyllium (Metamucil, Perdiem Fiber), methylcellulose (Citrucel), guar gum (Benefiber), and

GOOD FIBER FINDS

Grains:
Bran cereals
Brown rice
Oat bran
Oatmeal
Popcorn
Wheat-flake cereals
Whole-wheat bread
Whole-wheat pasta
Vegetables:
Baked potato, with skin
Broccoli
Brussels sprouts
Cabbage
Carrots
Corn
Green peas
Squash
Fruits:
Apples, with skin
Bananas

Berries (strawberries,
    blueberries, rasp-
    berries)
Dried apricots
Oranges
Pears
Prunes
Raisins
**Dried Beans and
Peas:**
Baked beans
Dried beans (kidney,
    pinto, navy)
Lentils
Split peas
Nuts and Seeds:
Almonds
Peanut butter
Peanuts
Sesame seeds
Sunflower seeds

fructan (FiberChoice). Unlike laxatives, they don't cause dependence, and as long as you take them as directed with plenty of fluids, they will encourage normal bowel function.

• If constipation or any other change in your usual bowel movements lasts more than three weeks, or if you notice blood on the toilet tissue or in the bowl, contact your doctor.

DIABETES

Diabetes may not generate the same sense of urgency or dread as cancer or heart disease, but it's a leading cause of blindness and amputations, and it contributes to more than 200,000 deaths each year. In excess of 18 million Americans suffer from diabetes, and nearly 16 million more show early warning signs of the disease. Older adults have always had the highest incidence, but alarming statistics show that diabetes is being diagnosed more and more in younger age groups, including children.

Almost everyone knows someone with diabetes, yet misinformation about it is common. Diabetes is *not* caused by eating too much sugar. But it's no coincidence that more than three-quarters of those with diabetes are overweight. And diet, along with physical activity and medication, is a cornerstone of managing the disease and fending off its potentially devastating complications.

Wayward Insulin

Diabetes develops when insulin can't do its job properly. Insulin is a hormone, or chemical messenger, that tells your body's cells to let glucose in. Glucose is the sugar that results from the breakdown of the food you eat. It circulates in your blood after a meal.

Without adequate amounts of insulin, the

cells won't get nourishment from the glucose waiting to enter, and the glucose just keeps circulating in the blood. That's why people with diabetes have high blood glucose levels.

The irony, if you have diabetes, is that although you have too much sugar in your blood, your cells are literally starving for lack of glucose. So they start breaking down fat for energy and, in the process, give off by-products called ketones. Having too many ketones in your blood is a sign you don't have enough insulin to move glucose into your hungry cells; the excess ketones are flushed out in your urine, which is why you may be instructed to test your urine for ketones. High levels of ketones in the blood can be toxic and lead to a serious condition called ketoacidosis.

Two Major Types

There are two major types of diabetes. Type 1, or insulin-dependent, diabetes (previously called juvenile diabetes), typically appears in childhood or young adulthood. If you have type 1 diabetes, you may be genetically prone to the disease, but its development may have been triggered by a virus or injury.

In type 1, the body simply does not produce enough insulin. Glucose sits outside the body's cells because there's no insulin on duty to let it in. So, people with type 1 diabetes must give themselves daily injections of insulin for the rest of their lives. To be most effective, injections must be carefully timed with meals and snacks.

Type 2 diabetes (sometimes referred to as non-insulin-dependent, or adult-onset, diabetes), typically strikes in middle age or later—but overweight, sedentary kids and younger adults are increasingly falling victim to this type. It is by far the most common type of diabetes. Your genes determine whether you are prone to this type of diabetes.

With type 2, there's usually plenty of insulin to go around, at least in the early and middle stages of the disease, but the cells don't respond to it. The effect is the same as with type 1: Little glucose enters the cells, so they starve, while sugar piles up in the bloodstream. We call this being "resistant" to insulin. A precursor to type 2 diabetes is a prediabetic condition called *insulin resistance*, or *impaired glucose tolerance*.

Your family tree will provide clues to whether you are likely to develop insulin resistance. But just because it runs in your family doesn't mean you will inevitably develop diabetes. If you are overweight, you may be able to prevent, or at least delay, the development of full-blown diabetes by losing weight. Being overweight doesn't cause diabetes, but if you have an inherited tendency toward diabetes, your extra weight may be enough to push you from insulin resistant into the diabetic range.

Just how important can weight loss be? Very. And you don't have to melt down to svelte to benefit. If you are overweight, losing only 5 to 10 percent of your body weight—about 10 to 20 pounds, on average—can significantly lessen the likelihood that you'll develop diabetes (and high blood pressure and heart disease, as well). For the severely obese, losing just half their excess weight can prevent diabetes. For someone who has already developed diabetes, losing just 10 to 20 pounds can mean lower blood sugar, blood pressure, and blood cholesterol levels!

The Telltale Signs

The classic signs of diabetes are insatiable thirst and excessive urination, to the point where the need to urinate may wake you several times each night. These two symptoms, caused by the need to get rid of excess sugar, are more noticeable in type 1 than in type 2. Other signs include fatigue, sores on your hands and feet that won't heal (because of poor blood flow), urinary tract infections, and blurry vision.

If you have type 1 diabetes, you may lose weight, because the glucose can't reach your cells. This does not usually happen with type 2 diabetes, because there's nearly always some insulin; it just isn't 100 percent effective. That's why the symptoms of type 2 are often less dramatic and more easily ignored. In fact, there may be no outward symptoms of type 2 at all.

Three-Pronged Therapy

No matter which type of diabetes you have, therapy to control blood glucose levels and delay, prevent, or minimize complications from diabetes involves three major weapons: diet, exercise, and medication (oral diabetes pills, insulin, or both). Type 1 diabetes must be treated with insulin injections, along with a proper diet and exercise program. People with type 2 diabetes may need diabetes pills and may even require insulin at some point, but the preferred therapeutic approach is to control blood glucose well enough with diet and exercise to avoid all that.

The range of oral diabetes medications and varieties of insulin available are beyond the scope of this book. But they have brought new hope, new freedom, and the promise of longer and healthier lives to millions of people with diabetes. Yet even for those who rely on medication to keep their diabetes well-managed, diet and exercise are essential components of their treatment regimens.

Exercise, one of the essential three prongs of diabetes therapy, functions a bit like insulin: It opens your cell doors to the glucose waiting in your blood. When you exercise, your blood glucose level decreases and you actually need less insulin, which is good. But it also means you must pay careful attention to your blood glucose levels and adjust your medication dose or your food intake accordingly, so that you don't have an insulin reaction.

An insulin reaction, or insulin shock, happens when your body has too much insulin—from injecting too much, from eating too little food, or from exercising too much without eating. Don't confuse it with diabetic coma, or ketoacidosis, which occurs if blood glucose levels go sky-high and eventually cause a toxic buildup of ketones (a problem more likely to happen in people with type 1 diabetes).

The symptoms of these two life-threatening conditions are easily con- fused, but the treatments for them are completely different, so you must familiarize yourself and your family and friends with the differences (see Know the Difference at left). Wearing a medic-alert bracelet or other identification is also a must. It's not unusual for bystanders to think someone having a diabetic reaction is simply drunk or on drugs.

Before you start an exercise session, therefore, eat a snack that contains a source of protein, such as half a turkey sandwich, yogurt, cheese, or milk. Also, keep a quick-acting sugar source with you to counteract the low blood glucose level that may occur during or after exercise (see Quick-Acting Sugars on the opposite page).

KNOW THE DIFFERENCE

Insulin reaction (insulin shock): Excessive sweating, rapid heartbeat, hunger, abdominal pain, weakness, fainting, clammy skin, pallor, tingling in mouth and fingers, irritability, blurred vision, drowsiness, headache. *You need sugar fast! Drink orange juice or regular soda or eat raisins or sugar cubes. Do not use chocolate; the fat slows sugar absorption.*

Ketoacidosis (diabetic coma): Nausea, vomiting, rapid breathing, sweet-smelling breath, dry mouth and skin, fixed and dilated pupils, coma. *Immediate medical assistance is required to lower blood sugar!*

QUICK-ACTING SUGARS

When your blood glucose drops too low, you need sugar that will be absorbed into your blood quickly. Try any of these (the amount you need varies according to your weight and level of activity):

Banana

Glucose tablets

Honey

Orange juice

Raisins

Regular soda

Sugar cubes

The Dietary Path to Tight Control

The aim in diabetes management is tight control—keeping blood glucose levels as close to normal as much of the time as possible. You want to avoid dramatic highs or lows, as well as perpetually above-normal levels of blood glucose. Together, these abnormal conditions cause damage to major arteries and smaller blood vessels, leading to diabetes complications—such as heart disease, kidney failure, blindness, nerve damage, and poor blood circulation—that can debilitate and kill.

Maintaining tight control may mean multiple injections of insulin or multiple doses of medication throughout the day. But for many people with type 2 diabetes, simply losing some weight by adding regular physical activity to their routine and manipulating the diet may be all that's needed to control blood glucose levels. For others, these lifestyle changes may allow the medications they take to work more effectively or to be used in smaller doses.

HERBS: THE FOURTH PRONG

Numerous studies have shown that a variety of herbs can help control blood sugar in people with diabetes. Most recently, the standout herb in these studies has been American ginseng root. Researchers have found that taking a supplement of 3 grams of American gingseng daily can lower blood sugar levels in people with diabetes by 10 percent or more. The best effect is when ginseng is taken after meals. It's not known exactly how ginseng works, but the results so far have been sufficiently promising that research clarifying this mystery is likely to be forthcoming. Consult a natural health care professional before combining American gingseng with diabetes medications or insulin, as this may cause blood sugar levels to drop too low. For further details about American ginseng, see the description of this valuable herb in Part III, page 195.

So what diet changes are required? The proper diet for people with diabetes is really just a healthy, well-balanced diet, based on pretty much the same heart-smart, anticancer diet recommendations that are suggested for everyone. In addition to making wise food choices, it's also *when* you eat that is important. When you have diabetes, you need to eat and check your blood glucose levels on a regular schedule; you also need to avoid skipping meals and overeating, both of which adversely affect your blood glucose control.

If you're looking for a specific diet plan, however,

you won't find it here. That's because there is no "standard" diet that works for everyone who has diabetes. Each person with diabetes needs individual dietary counseling. It's the only way that your dietary plan can be personalized to fit *your* body's calorie needs, taking into account how *your* blood glucose levels react to different foods in different amounts, how much and when *you* exercise, and what *your* food preferences, schedule, and habits are.

Consult with a registered dietitian to develop a diet and meal plan that suits your body's needs and your tastes and lifestyle. With it, you will gradually learn to adjust and keep track of what and when you eat—and recognize how the foods you choose affect your blood glucose levels—to help tighten control of your diabetes. You and your dietitian may even design a plan that helps you with other health goals at the same time, such as losing excess body fat or lowering blood pressure or blood cholesterol levels. At its most basic level, such a plan is likely to follow these American Diabetes Association guidelines:

Carbohydrate: This should make up the bulk of your daily calories. Most of your choices should come from whole grains, fruits, vegetables, legumes, and low-fat dairy products. Go easy on refined carbohydrates, such as sugar, white bread, and baked goods. Sugar is not taboo; just be sure to figure it into your total daily carbohydrate allowance or compensate with additional insulin or other glucose-lowering medication, if needed.

AN ALTERNATIVE APPROACH

A nontraditional diet approach may be right for some people with diabetes who also have high blood levels of triglycerides (the storage form of fat) and low blood levels of "good" HDL cholesterol. In some people, the high-carbohydrate diet described on pages 61 to 63 raises triglycerides and lowers HDLs, which is undesirable because this may increase heart-disease risk. A compromise diet consists of cutting back on total carbohydrates and replacing some of those calories with fat, on the condition that those extra fat calories come from monounsaturated fats, such as olive and canola oils. The best advice for you is to be sure your health care provider monitors your blood lipid (fat) levels if you are on a high-carbohydrate diet and pays particular attention to your triglyceride and HDL levels. That way, if they move in the wrong direction, the two of you can decide if you should cut back on carbohydrates and increase your intake of monounsaturated fats.

You may hear about choosing carbohydrate foods based on their glycemic response. This system for rating foods tells you how your blood glucose may react after eating individual foods. Many diabetes professionals do not suggest that you rely solely on this system for making food choices, however, because the total amount of sugars and starches you get from meals and snacks is considered more important than their source or type.

Even if you don't use the glycemic-response

system, you will almost certainly be asked by your dietitian and/or doctor to keep a record of the foods—and specifically the grams of carbohydrate—in your meals and snacks. That's because carbohydrate has the greatest, most direct effect on your blood glucose levels, compared to the effects of fat and protein, the other primary nutrients in food. In time, you may learn to adjust the amount and type of carbohydrate you eat at each meal to tightly control your blood glucose levels.

Protein: The recommendation for protein—15 to 20 percent of a day's total calories—is the same for people with or without diabetes. That amounts to about 45 to 50 grams of protein a day for a typical woman weighing between 125 and 140 pounds and about 60 to 65 grams a day for a typical man weighing between 165 and 180 pounds.

Fat: Keep your intake at 30 percent or less of daily calories. It's most important to limit saturated fats; emphasize monounsaturated or polyunsaturated fats instead.

Cholesterol: Limit your dietary intake to 300 milligrams a day.

Sodium: Limit your daily sodium intake to 2,300 milligrams, especially if your blood pressure is high. Replace your saltshaker with salt-free seasonings and fresh herbs and spices, and look for canned and processed foods that are "low in sodium" or have "no added salt."

Fiber: Try to get at least 25 grams of fiber a day. You can get it from fruits, vegetables, whole grains, and legumes.

DIVERTICULAR DISEASE

�֍ ✖ ✖

For some people with diverticular disease, the pain can seem unbearable. For others, it may be a minor nuisance. Diverticular disease encompasses two conditions—diverticulosis and diverticulitis. In diverticulosis, small areas of the intestinal lining balloon out through weak areas of the intestinal wall, forming little pouches called diverticula. The condition grows more common with age. Some 10 percent of Americans over age 40 have diverticulosis, and about half of those over age 60 do, too. If these pouches become irritated and infected, the condition is known as diverticulitis and can trigger constipation or diarrhea, gas, abdominal pain, fever, and mucus and blood in the stools. Diverticulitis occurs in 10 to 25 percent of people with diverticulosis.

Although there is no definitive answer to why the pouches develop in the first place, many experts believe diverticula form as a result of the increased pressure needed to eliminate the small, hard stools characteristic of a low-fiber diet.

A Diverticular Diet

Ironically, in years past, the diet recommended for folks with diverticulosis was low in fiber. It was thought that "roughage" might irritate the diverticular pouches and trigger inflammation. Today, however, we know it's the absolute wrong approach.

People who eat a low-fiber diet with few whole grains, fruits, and vegetables are actually *more* likely to develop diverticular disease than those who eat a high-fiber one.

To help prevent the disease or keep it under control, you should gradually add fiber to your diet and drink plenty of fluids. Eating regular meals, being physically active, getting enough rest, and keeping stress under control are also recommended.

A high-fiber diet is recommended to reduce constipation and the corresponding pressure required to move waste through the intestines. The goal is to find the amount of fiber that allows you to have regular, easy-to-pass bowel movements; it's probably in the range of 20 to 35 grams of fiber daily. (See the chart on page 66 for good fiber choices.) If you have not been eating much fiber, increase your intake gradually. If you get overzealous, you could make matters worse—too much fiber too fast may cause gas and bloating.

The age-old advice for people with diverticulosis was to avoid *all* nuts, seeds, and hulls. It is now recommended that only foods that are sharp, hard, or large enough to irritate or get caught in the diverticula be avoided. These include nuts, popcorn hulls, and sunflower, pumpkin, caraway, and sesame seeds. Other foods with small, soft seeds are generally not a problem; these include tomatoes, zucchini, cucumbers, strawberries, raspberries, and poppy seeds. If you have regular bowel movements that pass easily, you will probably be able to

FRUITS

Food	Portion	Fiber
Apple, raw, with skin	1 medium	4 grams
Peach, raw	1 medium	2 grams
Pear, raw	1 medium	4 grams
Tangerine, raw	1 medium	2 grams

VEGETABLES

Asparagus, fresh, cooked	4 spears	1 gram
Beans, baked, canned, plain	½ cup	6.5 grams
Beans, kidney, fresh, cooked	½ cup	8 grams
Beans, lima, fresh, cooked	½ cup	6.5 grams
Broccoli, fresh, cooked	½ cup	2.5 grams
Brussels sprouts, cooked	½ cup	2 grams
Cabbage, shredded, raw	1 cup	2 grams
Carrots, fresh, cooked	½ cup	2.5 grams
Cauliflower, fresh, cooked	½ cup	1.5 grams
Lettuce, romaine	1 cup	1 gram
Potato, baked, with skin	1 medium	5 grams
Potato, fresh, cooked	1	3 grams
Spinach, fresh, cooked	½ cup	2 grams
Squash, summer, cooked	1 cup	3 grams
Squash, winter, cooked	1 cup	6 grams
Tomato, raw	1	1 gram

GRAINS

Bread, whole-wheat	1 slice	2 grams
Cereal, 100% bran	½ cup	8–15 grams
Cereal, bran-flake	¾ cup	5 grams
Oatmeal, plain, cooked	¾ cup	3 grams
Rice, brown, cooked	1 cup	2.5 grams
Rice, white, cooked	1 cup	1 gram

handle most foods. If you find a certain food bothers you, it might be best to avoid it.

When It Gets Worse

If diverticulosis progresses to diverticulitis, bed rest, pain relievers, and antibiotics for the infection are usually the order of the day. The pain may come on suddenly and mimic appendicitis, although diverticulitis pain usually occurs on the left side, or the pain may build up slowly over a period of days. The real danger with diverticulitis is that pouches may rupture and spill bowel contents into the pelvic cavity. This can cause serious bodywide infection. More often, however, the pouches become inflamed without actually rupturing and disrupt your normal bowel function. Occasionally, diverticulitis leads to obstruction, hemorrhage, abscess, or a leak through the bowel wall. These are serious conditions requiring immediate medical and perhaps surgical treatment. (If you have been diagnosed with diverticulosis, be sure you discuss with your doctor what to do in the event of a flare-up and what symptoms signal the need for immediate medical attention.)

If you suspect your diverticulosis has progressed to diverticulitis, call your doctor and stick with a liquid or very low-fiber diet. When your symptoms subside, a high-fiber diet may be gradually reintroduced. If your diverticulitis is severe, you may need hospitalization and intravenous antibiotics. In some cases, surgery may be necessary.

GALLBLADDER PROBLEMS

✳ ✳ ✳

Some 20 million Americans live with gallstones, but only a small percentage experience symptoms, and even fewer have recurrent problems. No one knows what causes gallbladder disease, but it's doubtful any one culprit is to blame. Several factors, including heredity, diet, hormones, overweight, and infections, likely play a role.

The medical terms for gallbladder disease are almost unpronounceable. Cholelithiasis (ko-le-li-THY-a-sis) refers to gallstones, and cholecystitis (ko-le-sis-TY-tis) to an inflamed gallbladder.

The Bile Mover

The gallbladder is a small, muscular, pear-shaped sac just under the right side of your liver. It can hold about a quarter cup of bile, a yellowish-green material produced by the liver. Bile is made of water, bile salts and acids, cholesterol, and phospholipids (compounds that help dissolve fats). Its main function is to help break up large globs of fat into smaller globs—the first step in digesting fat.

A healthy gallbladder keeps bile moving, making stone formation unlikely. However, if something goes awry, the sludgelike contents of the gallbladder can crystalize, creating a gallstone. The most common type of gallstone forms when bile becomes supersaturated and cholesterol crystals form. Stones can grow quite large, and your gallbladder may contain hundreds of them. They can be detected through a special X-ray called a cholecystogram.

Secret Stones

Most people with gallstones don't know they have them. These symptomless stones probably float freely in the gallbladder. But if a stone settles in the duct that leads to the small intestine, it will let its presence be known. If the stone is large enough to block the flow of bile out of the duct, it will trigger severe pain and nausea, maybe even vomiting, fever, bloating, belching, and jaundice.

The most serious scenario is when pressure builds in the gallbladder to the point where it bursts. Left untreated, this can lead to peritonitis, a severe infection of the abdominal cavity. A blocked gallbladder duct can also damage your pancreas and liver. But all this is unlikely. If you see a doctor when symptoms appear, the gallbladder will probably be removed before your condition reaches this critical point.

Who Gets Stones?

Women are much more likely than men to develop gallstones. This is because estrogen stimulates the liver to remove more cholesterol from the blood and divert it into the bile, where it can form gallstones. Several large studies have shown that hormone replacement therapy significantly increases the risk of gallstones. Excess estrogen from pregnancy or birth control pills can also increase cholesterol levels in bile.

Getting older carries a greater risk of gallbladder

disease. But age isn't the only risk factor. Other high-risk groups include overweight women, Native Americans from the southwestern United States (such as the Pima), Mexican Americans, and people with diabetes. Taking drugs to lower cholesterol can also increase risk.

The Diet Connection

Experts say some, though not all, gallbladder disease can be prevented, and diet appears to play a crucial role. The composition of your bile strongly affects your risk of developing gallstones. And what you eat influences bile composition.

The strongest diet connection relates to eating too much. Research has found, at least in women, that the heavier you are, the higher your gallstone risk. Even being moderately overweight almost doubles your risk. While losing weight can decrease your risk in the long run, you need to take it slowly. Ironically, rapid weight loss is a suspect in gallstone formation.

Very low-fat diets may also be risky. Without enough fat to stimulate it, the gallbladder becomes inactive, allowing stones to form. Some studies

GOOD FOODS TO CHOOSE

• High-fiber foods, such as whole-grain breads and cereals, vegetables, fruits, and legumes

• Vitamin-C-rich foods, such as oranges, strawberries, kiwi, mangoes, tomatoes, broccoli, cauliflower, and potatoes

have found a lower risk for gallstones in people who eat foods high in monounsaturated fats (olive and canola oils) or omega-3 fatty acids (canola, flaxseed, and fish oils). While there is some speculation that eating fat helps improve liver clearance of cholesterol and bile, some people with gallstones experience discomfort following fatty meals. You should be the judge of what triggers your symptoms and stay away from foods that produce problems for you.

High-fiber diets seem to offer some protection against gallstones. And a small protective effect has been seen in women who eat a lot of vegetables. Preliminary research suggests other foods may offer protection, including alcohol in small amounts (one ounce per day), foods with vitamin C, and coffee (two to four cups a day). Regular, vigorous exercise also may reduce gallstone risk. Though cholesterol is a major component of stones, the amount in your diet probably has little, if any, effect on whether you develop gallstones.

WHEN DIET ISN'T ENOUGH

Doctors use a variety of treatments to provide some degree of relief from chronic gallbladder disease, but the standard treatment is to remove the organ. Once the gallbladder is removed, bile flows from the liver into the small intestine, instead of being stored in the gallbladder. Most people can resume a normal diet after having their gallbladder removed.

HEART DISEASE AND STROKE

✂ ✂ ✂

Many ingredients go into the "recipe" for a heart attack or stroke. Some you're born with. Some you acquire as you age. Fortunately, some of them you can change.

The Cholesterol Factor

You are measuring a potential risk factor, or "ingredient," for heart disease and stroke when you have your blood cholesterol or blood pressure checked. High blood pressure, as a risk factor and a disease in itself, is discussed in its own section, so we'll focus on blood cholesterol levels here.

Your body needs a small amount of cholesterol to function properly, but too much can cause serious heart and blood-vessel trou-ble. For cholesterol to move through the blood-stream, it must be attached to a fatty substance called a lipoprotein. There are two basic kinds of these cholesterol transporters: high-density lipoproteins, or HDLs, and low-density lipoproteins, or LDLs. The HDLs are considered helpful, because they remove excess cholesterol in the blood, preventing it from clogging arteries. LDLs, by contrast, tend to deposit excess cholesterol in blood vessels, where it can block the flow of blood to the heart and brain.

Oxidized or rancid LDL cholesterol is the major form of cholesterol that deposits in the arteries, which helps explain the importance of antioxidant nutrients, including vitamins C and E, beta carotene, and selenium. These antioxidants can help slow or prevent oxidative damage in the body.

Total cholesterol is usually measured when blood cholesterol is checked, because it is easier to test for than are the individual lipoproteins. For years it's been known that the higher your total cholesterol, the greater your chances of suffering a heart attack or stroke. In general, you want total cholesterol below 200 mg/dL. Having a reading above 240 means you're entering the danger zone.

A total cholesterol reading tells you the sum of your HDLs and LDLs, but it doesn't tell you how much you have of each. Because it's good to have a lot of HDLs in your blood but bad to have a lot of LDLs, this is important information to know. So, while your total cholesterol number is useful, it isn't the whole story. That's why the latest recommendations from the National Cholesterol Education Program say that a complete lipoprotein profile (which includes total cholesterol, LDLs, HDLs, and triglycerides) is the preferred initial test for checking your heart-disease risk. In fact, all adults 20 years of age or older should have a fasting lipoprotein profile done once every five years. Here's how to assess your levels:

Total Cholesterol

When your total cholesterol is high, your risk for heart disease goes up.

- Less than 200 mg/dL is desirable

- 200 to 239 mg/dL is borderline high

- 240 mg/dL and above is high

LDL Cholesterol

LDL cholesterol builds up in the arteries and may block the flow of blood. It is dangerous at high levels.

- Less than 100 mg/dL is optimal

- 100 to 129 mg/dL is near optimal

- 130 to 159 mg/dL is borderline high

- 160 to 189 mg/dL is high

- 190 mg/dL is very high

HDL Cholesterol

This beneficial lipoprotein carries cholesterol away from the arteries and back to the liver, where it can be broken down. There-fore, higher HDL numbers are better.

- Less than 40 mg/dL is low and a major risk factor for heart disease

- 40 to 59 mg/dL is good

- 60 mg/dL and above is protective and low-ers your risk

Triglycerides

Triglycerides are a form of fat in your blood. The higher the number, the greater your risk.

- 150 to 199 mg/dL is borderline high

- 200 to 499 mg/dL is high

- ≥500 mg/dL is very high

Beyond Cholesterol

Your total blood choles-terol level is a very impor-tant factor in assessing

UNDERSTANDING TRIGLYCERIDES

In the past, experts weren't sure what to make of high triglyceride levels. More recently, however, researchers have learned that high levels of triglycerides, the body's storage form of the fat that you eat, are definitely not good. In fact, high triglyceride levels are now considered an independent risk factor for heart disease and heart attack.

What causes triglyceride levels to rise? People with high triglyceride levels typically have a few things in common, including excess weight, physical inactivity, smoking, excess alcohol intake, a diet high in carbohydrates (>60 percent of calories from carbs), certain other diseases (such as diabetes and kidney disease), certain medications, and a family history of high triglyceride levels.

The recommended treatment to lower them depends on the causes. Most often, the emphasis is placed on quitting smoking, losing weight, and increasing physical activity. Changes in diet, such as avoiding alcohol and limiting refined carbohydrates (sugars and sweets, white breads and other refined grains, etc.), may also be in order. If these strategies don't work, or if the triglycerides are very high, drug therapy may be necessary.

your risk for heart disease and stroke. And, as you'll learn, what you eat can influence that level. But there are major risk factors other than total cholesterol level to be considered as well (some of these can also be affected by diet). The more risk factors you have, the greater your chances of having a heart attack or stroke. These other risk factors include

- Diabetes

- Low HDL level

- High triglyceride level

- Overweight

- Sedentary lifestyle

- Smoking

- High blood pressure (140/90 mmHg or above or use of blood-pressure medication)

- Family history of early heart disease (before age 55 in your father or brother; before age 65 in your mother or sister)

- Age (risk increases in men 45 and older, women 55 and older)

How a Heart Attack Begins

We're not talking about the moment you feel the crushing weight in your chest and the pain radiating down your arm. We mean when it really begins, years before. Trouble starts when LDL cholesterol in the bloodstream finds "nicks" in the blood-vessel walls—places to grab onto. The LDLs cling to these weak spots and attract other substances such as minerals and cell debris to form plaque, and they also become oxidized. Plaque is what hardens along the inside of your blood-vessel walls, narrowing the diameter through which blood can flow. The more LDLs you have floating around, the more there are to initiate the plaque process.

Experts think this process starts in the teenage years or young adulthood, as something they call fatty streaks. Over time, the plaque grows larger, it becomes fibrous, and it calcifies, almost like scar tissue, literally "hardening" your arteries. Eventually, it can completely block an artery leading to the heart, preventing the flow of blood and oxygen. If this happens in a small artery or if the blockage in a major artery is incomplete, you may experience only chest pain, called angina. But if complete blockage occurs in one of the major arteries that feed your heart, you'll have a heart attack, what doctors refer to as a myocardial infarction, or an MI.

The Devastating Stroke

A stroke occurs when a blood vessel leading to the brain either bursts or becomes clogged by a clot. The rupture or blockage prevents oxygen- and nutrient-rich blood from reaching the brain. Deprived of oxygen, nerve cells in the brain die within minutes.

Approximately 80 percent of strokes result from the kind of clots that cause heart attacks. The rest are caused by hemorrhages; these "bleeding strokes" occur when vessels rupture, spilling blood into the brain. The risk of death is much greater with a bleeding stroke than with one from a clot. In either type, brain cells may die, possibly resulting in permanent paralysis and loss of speech or memory.

Prevention Starts Now

It makes sense that if heart and blood-vessel diseases

RECOGNIZING A STROKE

Signs of a stroke are sometimes ignored. A stroke can come on suddenly, and treatment can be more effective if given quickly. Every minute counts, so learn to recognize the symptoms:

• Sudden numbness or weakness of the face, arm, or leg, especially on only one side of the body

• Sudden confusion or trouble speaking or understanding speech

• Sudden difficulty seeing with one or both eyes

• Sudden trouble walking, dizziness, or loss of balance or coordination

• Sudden, severe headache with no known cause

Also be aware of transient ischemic attacks (TIAs), small warning strokes that produce strokelike symptoms but no lasting damage. Recognizing and treating TIAs can reduce your risk of having a major stroke. They should never be ignored.

start early, prevention should, too. Don't put it off—you may not get an early warning. For one of every four people who suffer a heart attack, sudden death is the first sign of the underlying damage.

Does that mean there's no point in mending your ways later in life? Absolutely not! Whether you've been lucky enough to survive a heart attack or stroke or you've yet to experience any symptoms at all, changing your lifestyle now can halt and may even reverse arterial blockage. It's more difficult now than when you were young. But the steps you need to take to prevent heart disease and stroke are the same no matter your age. Fortunately, there's a lot you can do.

True, you can't change the genes you were born with; some people are just more prone to heart disease. But if you know that heart disease runs in your family, you have an even greater incentive to take as many steps as possible to fight it.

What else can't you change? Time marches forward for all of us, so the added risk as we age is a given. If you're a man, however, you're more vulnerable to heart and blood-vessel disease at an earlier age. That doesn't mean women should feel immune. After menopause, the rate of heart and blood-vessel diseases quickly evens out. And women at this stage in life are actually more likely to *die* if they suffer a heart attack or stroke.

So what *can* you change? Plenty. We'll touch on some important nondietary steps, but as the topic of this book is food and healing, we'll focus primarily on the myriad dietary changes that may make a difference.

"TLC" for a Healthy Heart

Your heart needs "tender loving care" to help it stay healthy for your lifetime. The National Cholesterol Education Program recommends Therapeutic Lifestyle Changes (TLC) to reduce the risk of heart disease. This multifaceted

THE TLC DIET

The National Cholesterol Education Program recommends Therapeutic Lifestyle Changes (TLC) for heart protection, including dietary modification based on the following daily goals*:

Total fat: 25 to 35 percent of total calories

Saturated fat: less than 7 percent of total calories

Polyunsaturated fat: up to 10 percent of total calories

Monounsaturated fat: up to 20 percent of total calories

Carbohydrate: 50 to 60 percent of total calories (mostly from vegetables, whole grains, fruits)

Fiber: 20 to 30 grams

Protein: approximately 15 percent of total calories

Cholesterol: less than 200 milligrams

Sodium: no more than 2,400 milligrams

Calories: enough to achieve or maintain a healthy weight

A registered dietitian can help you create a meal plan that fits within these guidelines.

approach stresses dietary change, weight loss, and increased physical activity.

Eating with your heart's health in mind means watching how much total fat, saturated fat, cholesterol, sodium, and calories you eat each day. The TLC Diet (which is outlined in the box on page 80) provides helpful guidelines from which to work.

If you're overweight, losing excess fat—even a relatively small amount—can help lower your total and LDL cholesterol levels, raise HDLs, and lower triglyceride levels. But be careful how you lose that weight. Crash diets are not the answer; slow and steady weight loss is your best bet. Why? First of all, you're more likely to keep it off. Second, research shows that extreme fluctuations in weight may actually add to the increased risk of heart attack that comes with being overweight in the first place.

Experts agree that physical activity should be part of everyone's daily routine, whether or not they have an increased risk of heart disease. Regular exercise can help you lower your LDLs, raise your HDLs, and lose weight. Aim for 30 minutes or more of physical activity on most, if not all, days of the week. Choose activities that raise your heart rate and use large muscles in your arms and/or legs, such as brisk walking, riding a bike, swimming, or dancing.

Before you make any major adjustments to your diet or activity level, however, get your doctor's approval. In addition, be sure any other health conditions that can affect your heart and blood vessels, such as high blood pressure and diabetes, are being properly treated.

A Cholesterol-Lowering Diet

People often say they're on a "low-cholesterol"

SOY GOOD

The evidence linking soy protein and heart-disease prevention was so compelling that the Food and Drug Administration approved a health claim for use on food labels stating: "25 grams of soy protein per day, as part of a diet low in saturated fat and cholesterol, may reduce the risk of heart disease."

For many, getting this much soy in the diet is a challenge. Fortunately, soy foods are becoming more widely available and versatile, so the choices extend far beyond the traditional tofu and soy milk. For instance, substitute soy flour for up to 30 percent of all-purpose flour in your recipe. Soy protein isolate, a powdered form of soy, can be added to a smoothie, sprinkled over cereal, or mixed in a casserole dish. Even easier and especially good for the soy wary are the veggie burgers, energy bars, breakfast cereals, and snack foods made from soy that are commonly available today.

diet. While that may be true, it's more important to be following a "cholesterol-lowering" diet. What's the difference? A diet that's low in cholesterol simply limits the amount of cholesterol you get from the foods you eat. But that's just one small part of a cholesterol-lowering diet, which aims to decrease the total amount of cholesterol in your blood.

The most important part of a cholesterol-lowering diet is limiting the amounts of saturated fat and total fat that you eat. Saturated fat increases your blood cholesterol levels even more than the cholesterol you eat does. (Animal fats tend to be high in saturated fats. Plant foods, on the other hand, tend to have more unsaturated fats; but there are exceptions, such as coconut oil, palm oil, and palm kernel oil, which are high in saturated fats.) Limiting the total amount of fat in your diet not only lowers your total blood cholesterol level, it can help you achieve and maintain a healthy weight. That's because a gram of fat provides more than twice the number of calories as does a gram of protein or carbohydrate.

Polyunsaturated fats are okay but are no longer revered, because besides lowering LDL, they also tend to lower HDL. Polyunsaturated fats are found in corn, soybean, safflower, and sunflower oils. Monounsaturated fats lower LDLs without lowering HDLs, so they are preferred as replacements for some of the saturated fat in your diet. Olive, canola, and peanut oils are rich in monounsaturates.

It's important to remember, however, that any fats that have been hydrogenated—forming *trans* fatty acids—are bad news when it comes to blood cholesterol levels. *Trans* fatty acids can raise blood cholesterol, possibly as much as saturated fats can. A product contains *trans* fats if you see "hydrogenated" or "partially hydrogenated" oils listed as primary ingredients. "*Trans* fat" is now listed on the Nutrition Facts panel of food products, too. But scientists are still trying to determine if there is an "acceptable" level of *trans* fats in food.

RED-MEAT REALITY

Red meat often gets a bad rap for being laden with fat and cholesterol. While it's true that you should be eating less total fat, saturated fat, and cholesterol, people often conclude that beef should be totally avoided and replaced by fish or skinless poultry.

However, several recent studies have concluded that eating lean red meat (beef, veal, and pork) is just as effective in reducing LDL cholesterol and raising HDL cholesterol as eating lean white meat (poultry and fish). A common misconception about red meat is that the majority of its fat is saturated; in fact, nearly half of the fat in lean beef is monounsaturated. This form of fat is believed to help lower blood cholesterol and reduce risk of heart disease. Beef also contains a type of saturated fat, called stearic acid, that doesn't raise cholesterol levels the way other saturated fats do. It just so happens to be one of the main saturated fats in chocolate, too. Just remember that higher-fat cuts of red meat are still high in calories and other cholesterol-raising saturated fats.

TIPS TO CUT FAT

• Make whole-grain foods the centerpiece of your meals. Add only two or three ounces of meat per person, either on the side or mixed with brown rice, potatoes, whole-wheat pasta and sauce, or couscous.

• Choose meat graded "select." There's less marbled fat that you can't cut out. Trim all visible fat, then broil or grill the meat, so fat drips away.

• Choose lean cuts of meat. For beef, pick anything with "round" or "loin" in its name, such as bottom round, top round, eye of round, top loin, sirloin, and tenderloin. For pork, choose center or tenderloin cuts. For ground meat, ask for ground round, or rinse ground meat in warm water first (to cut fat content).

• Remove skin from poultry; it's where most of the fat is. You can keep it on during cooking to hold in juices, but remove it before eating.

• Drink fat-free (skim) or 1 percent milk. Switching from whole to fat-free milk saves more than 60 calories and almost 8 grams of fat per cup. Can't go cold turkey? First switch to 2 percent, then to 1 percent, then to skim, even mixing 2 percent and 1 percent for a while if necessary. Also, try low-fat or nonfat versions of other dairy products, such as yogurt, cottage cheese, American and hard cheeses, and buttermilk.

• Regular sour cream has about one-fifth the calories of butter or margarine, so it's a better choice for topping potatoes. And now you can try fat-free varieties for greater fat savings. Another option is to use plain, drained, nonfat yogurt mixed with some chives instead.

SPREADING CONFUSION?

Given the choice of butter, margarine, or one of the many buttery spreads, which do you choose? Although butter and stick margarine are nearly equal in total fat, butter is higher in saturated fat, while stick margarine is higher in *trans* fat. But butter tops out with the highest total amount of saturated and *trans* fat, and it contains cholesterol, too. Choose soft margarines (liquid or tub varieties) over harder stick forms for even less saturated and *trans* fats. Some tub margarines are even *trans*-fat free (check labels to find them).

Newer products on the shelves are designed to lower elevated blood cholesterol levels. These contain plant stanols or sterols, substances derived from vegetable oils, corn, and beans. When these spreads are used in recommended amounts, they may help lower LDL levels. They work by reducing the body's absorption of cholesterol. Recommended amounts are about 2 tablespoons per day in place of other fats. They can be more expensive, however.

Rather than any of these spreads, you might try using one of the butter-flavored products that you spray or sprinkle on food. These offer buttery flavor with very little or no fat. Spray butter flavor on your corn on the cob, sprinkle buttery powder on steamy vegetables, or use a spritzer filled with olive oil to spray vegetables as you roast them. You can also spray pans to coat them.

• Try evaporated skim milk as a fat-free coffee creamer. Chances are, you won't be able to tell the difference between it and the stuff you usually pour into your coffee at work or even at home. Why bother? Well, consider this: Half-and-half gets 78 percent of its calories from fat, while many nondairy creamers or "coffee lighteners" get 90 percent of theirs from fat. What's more, a lot of nondairy powdered creamers are made with saturated palm or coconut oil.

• Make simple substitutions for a big fat difference: Switch to low-fat, reduced-fat, or fat-free versions of mayonnaise, salad dressing, sour cream, cream cheese, and other cheese products.

• Read labels to avoid highly saturated coconut and palm-kernel oils. Beware of foods listing partially hydrogenated oil as the first or second ingredient.

• If you make soup or gravy, leave enough time to chill it beforehand, so you can skim off the fat that congeals on top.

• When eating out, ask for meats and fish to be broiled or grilled; avoid sautéed and fried items. Order sauces and dressings on the side. Dip your fork into them so they just coat the tines. Then spear your food.

• On menus, watch for words that spell trouble: Alfredo, au gratin, béarnaise, béchamel, beurre blanc, escalloped, hollandaise, and parmigiana.

• When it's time for dessert, opt for sorbet, fruit, or ice milk for flavor without loads of fat. Or, if you really want that rich dessert, share it with your dining companions.

• For cooking/baking, use nonstick vegetable spray in place of a tablespoon of butter or margarine to save about 10 grams of fat and 92 calories.

• Season potatoes, vegetables, pastas, and rice with butter-flavored granules. One teaspoon adds only 8 calories but replaces the 108 calories and 12 grams of fat in a tablespoon of butter.

• Cut oil by half in recipes; often, it won't change how the dish turns out.

OAT BRAN & BEYOND

You may have thought the oat-bran-as-heart-food phenomenon died out at the end of the '80s. But to borrow from Mark Twain, reports of its demise were greatly exaggerated. Oat bran has repeatedly been shown to help lower cholesterol levels because of its soluble-fiber content.

There are a few caveats, however. It's most helpful to people whose cholesterol levels are above 240 mg/dL. And you need to eat quite a bit to notice a difference. One study found that three grams of soluble fiber a day—a large bowl of oat bran cereal or three packets of instant oatmeal—reduced high blood cholesterol levels by five or six points beyond what a low-fat, low-cholesterol diet could do.

Increasing fiber by any amount, regardless of the type, provides benefits when it takes the place of more-refined foods high in fat and calories. Fiber is found in fruits, vegeta-

THE HOMOCYSTEINE CONNECTION

Too much homocysteine, an amino acid in the blood, has been linked to a higher risk of heart disease and stroke. Evidence suggests that homocysteine may promote atherosclerosis (fatty deposits in blood vessels) by damaging the inner lining of arteries and promoting clots. Homocysteine levels are strongly influenced by diet and genetic factors. Folic acid and other B vitamins help break down homocysteine in the body. Several studies found that higher levels of these B vitamins may help lower concentrations of homocysteine. The greatest effects result from food sources of these vitamins. However, no controlled treatment study has shown that supplementation with B vitamins affects the development or recurrence of cardiovascular disease. To help counteract elevated homocysteine levels, try eating more foods rich in folate (see page 18), foods enriched with folic acid (see page 17), and foods rich in vitamin B_{12} (all animal products).

bles, legumes, nuts, and whole-grain breads, cereals, and pastas.

Antioxidant Protection

You remember antioxidants—those nutrients that fend off dangerous free radicals that form whenever oxidation occurs? (See Cancer profile, page 21.) Research has shown them to help prevent heart disease, too, most likely because they prevent or reverse oxidation of LDLs in artery-hardening plaques. Free-radical damage to your arteries and heart can be deterred by antioxidant nutrients— namely beta-carotene and other carotenoids, vitamin C, and vitamin E.

Still being studied is what amounts of these antioxidants are needed to provide the greatest benefits. To get enough vitamin E to act as an antioxidant, you probably need a supplement. But you can get plenty of vitamin C, beta-carotene, and other substances with antioxidant properties from foods, especially by eating a wide variety of fruits and vegetables.

Fishing for Heart Help

Fish oils made big news a few years back, then seemed to fade from the limelight. But the evidence that they help prevent heart disease remains. What has been tempered is the enthusiasm for fish-oil supplements. No one is really sure how much helps, and too much can cause bleeding problems. So, the emphasis is on eating fish. In fact, the American Heart Association now recommends two weekly servings of fish.

Just what do fish oils, known as omega-3 fatty acids, do? This polyunsaturated fat has been found to prolong blood-clotting time, making blockage inside blood vessels less likely. It may also lower blood triglyceride levels and blood pressure. Fish aren't the only source of omega-3s. Other foods that boast omega-3s include flax, soy, walnut, and canola oils. (See pages 12–13 for other good sources of omega-3s.)

HEMORRHOIDS

✖ ✖ ✖

You may think hemorrhoids are a problem of the modern world, born of our refined diet and sedentary ways. And it's true they're one of the most common problems doctors encounter today. But while our "civilized" lifestyle certainly contributes to the condition, people have been suffering from hemorrhoids, or "piles" as they used to be called, for centuries. And then as now, the cause and best remedies remain the same.

It's All About Pressure

Hemorrhoids are caused by stress on the veins in the rectum. That pressure can come from many sources, including standing upright for long periods; pregnancy; straining or pushing because of constipation, diarrhea, or trying to force a bowel movement; sitting too long; obesity; and even prolonged coughing and sneezing.

Too much pressure can cause veins in the rectum and anus to swell and stretch out of shape. Internal hemorrhoids form just under the tissue that lines the inside of the rectum. They are not visible unless they become so big they prolapse, or fall down and protrude through the anus. External hemorrhoids form outside the rectum, in the veins surrounding the anus.

Either type of hemorrhoid can bleed, although external ones are more prone to bleeding, because they're easily irritated. The itching, burning, and pain typically associated with hemorrhoids result from the external variety. If an internal hemorrhoid develops a fissure—a tear or ulcer in the anal canal—or forms a blood clot, it can cause severe pain. But normally, internal hemorrhoids don't burn or itch, because there are no nerve endings in the lining of the rectum. Indeed, in 1991 the Food and Drug Administration banned 30 over-the-counter hemorrhoid preparations from the market as unsafe or ineffective because they were purportedly designed to relieve discomfort *inside* the rectum. Now, products must be labeled "for external use only."

Almost all rectal bleeding is due to hemorrhoids, but because such bleeding can, in rare instances, signal other serious disease, notably colon cancer, you should always consult a doctor if you spot blood in the toilet or on the toilet tissue after you wipe if that bleeding lasts more than a day. External hemorrhoids are easily diagnosed, but to detect internal hemorrhoids, a doctor may need to use a special instrument called a proctoscope to look inside the rectum.

Preventing "Piles"

Hemorrhoids aren't dangerous. They don't lead to cancer or other serious conditions. They rarely bleed enough to cause anemia. In fact, they often cause no symptoms at all. Still, they can be extremely uncomfortable, and most people would just as soon not have them.

Prevention, of course, is the preferred method of dealing with them. One of the best ways to prevent hemorrhoids is to develop good bowel, exercise, and dietary habits when you're young. But it's never too late.

Good bowel habits mean going only when you have the urge, not necessarily every morning, and not holding it in until a more convenient time. There are limits to this, of course, but in general, try to go when nature calls. This develops what doctors call good bowel "tone." A sure way to ruin good tone is to rely on laxatives. Overuse makes your intestinal muscles eventually "forget" how to work. The result is increasing difficulty passing a stool, which in turn requires more straining. Remember, everyone's body has a different rhythm; some people may go twice a day, but it's perfectly normal if you only have bowel movements every three days. Avoid labeling yourself as constipated unless you have bothersome symptoms.

Try to avoid sitting too much—especially on the toilet. This position relaxes your rectal muscles, allowing blood to fill your veins and creating pressure. Physical activity, on the other hand, stimulates all your muscles, including those in the rectum, helping prevent constipation.

Fixing the Problem

Constipation is the classic cause of hemorrhoids, but diarrhea can create similar pressure, as well. Both, fortunately, can be treated with a high-fiber diet. Bran, specifically wheat

HEMORRHOID PREVENTION

• Eat a high-fiber diet emphasizing wheat bran. Include five daily servings of fruits and vegetables, opt for whole over refined grains, and make beans a mainstay of meals. If necessary, use a bulk softener but not a laxative.

• Drink lots of fluids, especially water. Set a goal of six to eight cups each day.

• Answer nature's call without delay whenever possible.

• Avoid straining when you're on the toilet. Wait for the urge to hit before you seat yourself on the "throne."

• Avoid sitting for long periods. Break it up with walks.

• Get some physical activity every day.

• Practice good hygiene. Wipe well but not excessively. Use water if necessary.

bran, is the time-honored cure-all, because it creates a bulky stool. Also look to other whole grains, fresh fruits and vegetables, and legumes. (See page 52 for a list of good fiber sources.) Add fiber gradually, though, so your body can adjust. If necessary, use an over-the-counter bulk-forming laxative, such as psyllium, but avoid other types of laxatives. It's best to get fiber from foods.

Drinking adequate fluids is also essential for good bowel function. Drink several cups—six to eight—of water each day. This is especially important if you're getting more fiber. Too much fiber can actually cause constipation if you're not also drinking adequate fluids.

HIGH BLOOD PRESSURE

If you knew there was a silent killer lurking, just waiting to strike its next victim, and that there was a one in four chance that victim might be you, would you be worried? Would you do everything you could to protect yourself? Of course you would. Well, it's a reality, and the silent killer is high blood pressure.

Why is high blood pressure, also called hypertension, so dangerous? Each time your heart beats, it pumps about two to three ounces of blood. When you're at rest, it does this 60 to 80 times per minute—or more than 100,000 times a day. All told, your heart pumps roughly 2,000 gallons of blood through the nearly 60,000 miles of blood vessels in your body every day! If the blood encounters any resistance as it flows through your blood vessels, it places more force against your artery walls—it increases your blood pressure—making your heart work even harder. That's why high blood pressure is a major risk factor for heart disease and stroke. It also increases the risk for developing kidney, eye, and nerve problems.

By the Numbers

The statistics are sobering: High blood pressure affects approximately 50 million people in the United States and more than one billion people worldwide. The higher your blood pressure, the greater your risk of heart attack, heart failure, stroke, and kidney disease.

At younger ages, more men suffer high blood pressure, but after age 65, more women are afflicted. And women account for more deaths from the disease. In fact, more than a quarter of adult American women have high blood pressure; after age 60, more than half of them do, with the percentages rising every year after that.

Scarier still are the statistics for minorities. African Americans are twice as likely to have high blood pressure and four times as likely to die from it. Puerto Ricans, Cuban Americans, and Mexican Americans are at greater risk, as well.

Check-Ins Required

If you have high blood pressure, odds are you have essential hypertension. That simply means doctors have no idea what caused it, although heredity and age likely played large roles. A small minority of people have secondary hypertension, meaning high blood pressure is a symptom of an underlying problem, which if corrected may remedy the high blood pressure. Essential hypertension, however, has no cure. You must treat it for life—with lifestyle changes and possibly drugs as well.

If hypertension has no symptoms, how do you know you have it? You must have your blood pressure checked regularly. Be sure to ask what your reading is every time, so you know if you're straying from your norm.

It's normal for blood pressure to vary throughout the day and to be affected by emotions, activity, and even eating. Often, just being in a doctor's office can raise blood pressure slightly. That's why it's so important to check it regularly. But one abnormal reading is nothing to worry about; high blood pressure is never diagnosed from a single reading.

What the Numbers Mean

Most of us are familiar enough with blood pressure readings to know that there are two numbers; the higher one is given first, "over" the lower number, like a fraction. But do you know what the numbers refer to?

Briefly, blood pressure is a measure of the force that your blood exerts against your blood-vessel walls. The higher number in the reading is called the systolic pressure—the pressure of the blood against the walls when the heart pumps. The lower number is the diastolic pressure—the pressure of the blood between the heart's beats.

The more resistance there is to smooth blood flow, the higher the numbers (and the higher the blood pressure) will be. If your arteries are clogged with plaque (for a discussion of how plaque forms and can then restrict the flow of blood through your arteries, see pages 76–77 in Heart Disease and Stroke), your heart has to work harder to pump blood throughout your body; there will be more resistance to the blood flow, hence a higher blood pressure. And that's not good. It can lead to a dangerously enlarged

TRANSLATING BLOOD PRESSURE

Here's how adult blood pressure readings are classified by the National Heart, Lung, and Blood Institute. You fall into the higher-risk category even if just one of the two numbers is in the higher range.

BLOOD PRESSURE READING

Systolic		Diastolic	Classification
<120		<80	normal
120–139	or	80–89	prehypertension
140–159	or	90–99	stage 1 hypertension
≥160	or	≥100	stage 2 hypertension

heart. The extra pressure on the blood-vessel walls can weaken them, too, making them susceptible to further injury. Blood flow to the body's organs may be slowed, as well, possibly leading to kidney disease, stroke, heart attack, or other life-threatening damage.

So what should your blood-pressure numbers be to avoid all that? In general, it's best if your systolic (upper) number is below 120 and your dia-stolic (lower) is below 80. There's a gray area of uncertain risk, sometimes referred to as "prehypertension," but scientists have agreed on certain cutoff points above which definite danger lurks. The National Heart, Lung, and Blood Institute (NHLBI) classifies blood pressure by systolic and diastolic levels to help doctors determine the best course of treatment (see Translating Blood Pressure, above).

Previously, doctors paid more attention to diastolic pressure, believing it to be a better indicator of potential trouble. Now, however, the recommendation is to give equal concern to both numbers (and ironically now the systolic number is actually thought to better predict the complications that arise from hypertension). For people who are diagnosed with hypertension, the aim is to reduce blood pressure below 140 over 90 and to less than 130 over 80 for people who also have diabetes or chronic kidney disease.

Dietary Changes to the Rescue

If you can prevent or lower high blood pressure, then you immediately and dramatically improve your chances for living free of heart disease, stroke, and kidney disease. It's that simple—and that important. Quitting smoking and losing weight are the two best and surest ways to reduce blood pressure—even if your blood pressure's not particularly high to begin with. Beyond those steps, experts recommend the following dietary changes to help prevent high blood pressure or keep it under control. (Be sure to consult your doctor, however, before making any significant dietary changes, especially if you are already taking medication to treat high blood pressure.)

Do the DASH. Research supported by the NHLBI led to the development of an eating plan that can prevent and help treat high blood pressure. The eating plan, known as DASH—named after a key study called Dietary

DASH TO BETTER HEALTH

Doing the DASH can help prevent or lower high blood pressure. To follow a DASH eating plan:

• Choose foods that are low in saturated fat, cholesterol, and total fat, such as lean meat, poultry, and fish.

• Eat plenty of fruits and vegetables; aim for eight to ten servings each day.

• Include two to three servings of low-fat or fat-free dairy foods each day.

• Choose whole-grain foods, such as 100 percent whole-wheat or whole-grain bread, cereal, and pasta.

• Eat nuts, seeds, and dried beans—four to five servings per week (one serving equals ⅓ cup or 1.5 ounces nuts, 2 tablespoons or ½ ounce seeds, or ½ cup cooked dried beans or peas).

• Go easy on added fats. Choose soft margarine, low-fat mayonnaise, light salad dressing, and unsaturated vegetable oils (such as olive, corn, canola, or safflower).

• Cut back on sweets and sugary beverages.

Approaches to Stop Hypertension—is low in saturated fat, cholesterol, and total fat and emphasizes fruits, vegetables, and low-fat dairy foods. It also includes whole-grain products, fish, poultry, and nuts, and it limits meat, sweets, and sugary beverages. This makes for a diet rich in magnesium, potassium, and calcium, as well as protein and fiber—a winning combination for lowering blood pressure.

(See DASH to Better Health on the facing page for more on this plan.)

Cut back on salt. Research using the DASH diet and different levels of dietary sodium confirmed what has been advised for many years—reducing dietary sodium and salt can help lower blood pressure. Some people, such as African Americans and the elderly, are especially sensitive to salt and sodium and should be particularly careful about how much they consume. Being sensitive to salt (or sodium) means you have a tendency to retain fluid when you take in too much salt, probably because of a defect in your kidneys' ability to get rid of sodium. Your body tries to dilute the sodium in the blood by conserving fluids. This forces your blood vessels to work extra hard to circulate the additional blood volume. The nerves on the blood vessels become overstimulated and start signaling the vessels to constrict (get smaller). This only makes it harder for the heart to pump, eventually causing blood pressure to rise.

Some people are less sensitive to the effects of excess salt. But because Americans use much more salt and sodium than they need—we consume anywhere from 6 to 20 grams of sodium a day—it's wise for most people to cut back. Your goal is to consume no more than 2.4 grams (2,300 milligrams) of sodium a day. That equals six grams (about a teaspoon) of table salt a day. Depending on how high your blood pressure is, your doctor may advise less. Remember, the six grams includes all salt and sodium consumed, including that used in cooking, at the table, and in processed and commercially prepared foods.

As much as 75 percent of the salt in our diets comes from processed foods. Only 10 percent of the salt we eat is there naturally, and about 15 percent is added during cooking and at the table. But since the taste for salt is learned—unlike our inborn taste for sugar—you can also learn to enjoy food with less salt. Retrain your taste buds and learn to enjoy food with less salt.

Before trying a salt substitute, check with your doctor. Many of them contain potassium chloride, and you may end up taking in too much potassium, which can be harmful, especially in combination with certain medications.

Rack up potassium.
Some people who have hypertension take thiazide diuretics that cause a loss of potassium, so they are told to eat a banana each day to replace it. But researchers now think extra potassium may be a good idea for everyone. Not only do we eat too much sodium, we take in too little potassium. It's the balance between sodium and potassium that is thought to be important to blood pressure.

Don't run out to buy potassium supplements, however. That could be dangerous. Both too much and too little potassium can trigger a heart attack. Stick to foods high in potassium to be safe; foods rich in potassium include bananas, oranges, potatoes, tomatoes, and milk. A caveat: If you have been diagnosed with high blood pressure and are taking a potassium-sparing diuretic (ask your doctor or pharmacist if you are unsure) or if you have kidney disease, first ask your doctor whether you need extra potassium.

Collect calcium. Your heart needs calcium to maintain its proper rhythm, and your kidneys need calcium to regulate your body's sodium/water balance. Research has shown, however, that people who have high blood pressure generally don't get enough dietary calcium. Other studies confirm that getting extra calcium can actually lower blood pressure. But that effect is not necessarily seen with calcium supplements. Rely, instead, on foods that are rich in calcium (see pages 122–123 for super food sources of calcium).

Go for garlic. Numerous researchers have pointed to garlic's ability to lower blood pressure. It also makes a fabulous flavor replacement when you're cutting back on salt.

Let fruits and vegetables reign. Vegetarians have a much lower incidence of high blood pressure. You, too, can benefit from this approach without becoming a vegetarian. Gradually increase your daily servings by sneaking in an extra serving or two at each meal. You will likely be eating less fat, more fiber, less salt, and more potassium—and you'll probably lose weight. Those benefits will help lower your blood pressure.

Curb the bad habits. Drinking, like smoking, is strongly associated with high blood pressure. Heavy drinkers probably double their risk of high blood pressure. The NHLBI recommends no more than two alcoholic drinks per day for men and no more than one per day for women. (One drink equals ½ ounce alcohol, the amount found in 12 ounces of beer, 5 ounces of wine, or 1½ ounces of 80-proof whiskey.)

Caffeine, however, doesn't appear to be associated with hypertension. While it can raise your blood pressure temporarily, your body adapts to the caffeine level if you routinely drink a certain amount of coffee, tea, or cola every day, and your blood pressure is no longer affected by that amount.

When Drugs Are Added

The myriad medications available for treating high blood pressure are beyond the scope of this book, and besides, most experts still consider lifestyle changes the frontline therapy for treating mild high blood pressure. Medications do play an important role when blood pressure rises into the danger zones of stage 1 and stage 2 high blood pressure. Still, medication does not take the place of lifestyle changes. A study of people with mild hypertension found the combination of medications and lifestyle changes (diet and exercise) more effective than either of them alone in preventing future heart attacks and strokes. And for people whose high blood pressure is more severe, lifestyle changes along with medication can result in smaller doses of the drugs, cutting both cost and risk of medication side effects.

IRRITABLE BOWEL SYNDROME

※ ※ ※

Bloating, distention, diarrhea alternating with constipation, and episodes of gut-wrenching pain are the hallmarks of irritable bowel syndrome, or IBS.

IBS is also known as spastic colon, irritable colon, and spastic colitis. Don't confuse it with IBD, or inflammatory bowel disease such as Crohn's disease and ulcerative colitis, serious conditions that sometimes require partial removal of the intestines.

A Distressing Disorder

IBS is not really a disease, and no one knows what causes it. It's called a "syndrome" because it is a collection of symptoms. It is diagnosed mainly by eliminating other, more serious conditions. And there is no cure.

One in five Americans has IBS, making it one of the most commonly diagnosed disorders. It occurs more often in women than in men, and it usually begins around age 20. You may actually suffer mild IBS symptoms for years before an acute attack sends you to the doctor for relief. The symptoms mimic those of more serious gastrointestinal, hormonal, and reproductive diseases and vary not only from person to person but in the same person from week to week. That makes diagnosis difficult and an effective treatment elusive.

Although IBS causes a great deal of discomfort

and distress, it does not permanently harm the intestines and does not lead to intestinal bleeding or any serious disease, such as cancer. Most people can control their symptoms with dietary adjustment, stress management, and medications prescribed by their physician. Unfortunately, for some people, IBS can be disabling. They may be unable to work, go to social events, or travel even short distances.

IBS Triggers

IBS symptoms are believed to be set off when something disrupts the normal functioning of the lower intestines. We don't know what triggers the malfunction, but it may be a combination of factors, including stress, hormonal fluctuations, biochemical disturbances, and possibly food sensitivities. The following have been associated with a worsening of IBS symptoms:

- large meals
- bloating from gas in the colon
- medicines
- wheat, rye, barley, chocolate, milk products, and alcohol
- drinks with caffeine
- stress, conflict, and emotional upsets

Research has shown that mild or "dormant" celiac disease may be responsible for the symptoms in a small group of people believed to have IBS. People with celiac disease cannot digest gluten (see Celiac Disease).

Diet Maneuvers

For many people, careful eating plays a key role in reducing IBS symptoms. Uncovering any foods that may trigger your IBS should be your first step. Keep a journal where you can record what you eat and any symptoms that follow. Then discuss your findings with your doctor. A registered dietitian can help you make changes to your diet.

Because symptoms of lactose intolerance can mimic those of IBS, try eliminating foods containing lactose (see Lactose Intolerance) for a couple of weeks to see if symptoms subside. Dairy products are an important source of calcium and other nutrients, so be sure to get adequate amounts of these nutrients from other foods or a supplement if you need to avoid dairy products to control your IBS (again, talk to your doctor or a registered dietitian).

In many cases, dietary fiber may lessen IBS symptoms, particularly constipation. However, it may not help pain or diarrhea. Whole-grain breads and cereals, fruits, and vegetables are good sources of fiber. *Gradually* increase your fiber intake to about 35 to 40 grams per day. With a gradual increase, most IBS sufferers handle high-fiber diets well. (See Constipation for more advice.)

Drinking six to eight glasses of water a day is important, especially if you have diarrhea or are increasing your fiber intake. But drinking carbonated beverages may cause gas and discomfort.

Chewing gum and eating too quickly can lead to swallowing air, which promotes gas. Large meals can cause cramping and diarrhea, so try eating smaller meals or eating smaller portions. It may also help to eat low-fat meals that are high in carbohydrates, such as pasta, rice, whole-grain breads and cereals (unless you have celiac disease), fruits, and vegetables.

If Diet Doesn't Do It

In addition to watching what you eat and minimizing stress, you may be able to control your symptoms by taking medication (laxatives, antidiarrheals, tranquilizers, or antidepressants), but you should discuss any drug treatment with your doctor first. Doctors generally hesitate to prescribe strong and sometimes addictive drugs (which may cause other digestive side effects) to treat IBS, because the root cause of the condition isn't understood, and it seldom leads to serious complications.

THE PEPPERMINT EFFECT

Before using medications, some of which have serious side effects, consider trying peppermint. Several studies have shown that it can reduce IBS symptoms, particularly when cramping and diarrhea are major problems. These studies have primarily involved capsules of peppermint essential oil (0.2 mL menthol) and have found that 1 capsule taken with each meal offers the best results. However, drinking 2 cups of strong peppermint tea (steep 2 tea bags in a covered cup of hot water for 20 minutes) with each meal is equally effective. Peppermint can exacerbate heartburn, but there are no other side effects.

KIDNEY STONES

✵ ✵ ✵

There's no romancing these stones. But with good nutrition, you may be able to prevent kidney stones from inflicting their pain on you.

Here's how stones are created: Substances that you get from your diet and that your body produces, including calcium and uric acid, dissolve in urine as it passes through the kidneys. If the urine becomes "supersaturated" with them and is unable to dissolve any more of the substances, the crystals settle and collect into clumps that accumulate into hard stones.

Approximately 10 percent of people develop kidney stones at some time in their lives. You're most likely to suffer stones if you are male, are 20 to 40 years old, have gout, or have a family history of kidney stones. But even if all of these conditions apply to you, drinking plenty of water may be enough to keep kidney stones at bay.

Like gallstones that go undiagnosed, kidney stones don't always cause problems. But when they grow large enough to block the flow of urine through the ureter (one of two tubes that allow urine to drain from the kidneys to the bladder), the pain can be excruciating. You're likely to first feel pain in the lower back, but it can spread to the thighs and groin. Other symptoms of the nasty infection a kidney stone can cause include nausea and vomiting, fever and chills, blood in the urine, and abdominal bloating.

Relief May Be Temporary

Getting rid of kidney stones used to be a much-dreaded surgical procedure followed by weeks of slow recovery. Today, thanks to lithotripsy, a high-tech procedure, invisible sound waves are passed through the body to pulverize stones to the consistency of sand. No anesthesia is required, and you can go home the same day.

Unfortunately, just because you made it through one bout with kidney stones doesn't mean you're home free. A repeat performance is likely. That's why prevention, as always, is the best medicine. Depending on the type of stone, you may be able to prevent recurrence by choosing the right diet.

HERBAL DIURETICS

Drinking plenty of water is the undisputed champion of kidney stone prevention. Some herbal teas, such as those made from the leaves of stinging nettles, may enhance the benefits of water by acting as natural diuretics. Nettle leaf has a long tradition of safely promoting urination, which keeps water moving so crystals can't form. It may also help maintain a kidney-stone-busting balance of electrolytes in the urine. Though further research is needed, drinking 2 to 3 cups of nettle leaf tea per day may help prevent kidney stones. Mix 1 to 2 tablespoons dried nettle leaf with 1 cup hot water and steep for 10 to 15 minutes.

Ironic Dietary Advice

Most kidney stones—about 90 percent—are made of calcium and oxalate, a chemical found in some plants. So, the standard advice doctors gave for years seemed reasonable: If you're at risk for stones, cut back on foods rich in calcium and oxalate.

But recent studies have shown foods high in calcium, including dairy foods, actually help prevent common stones. Why? It seems the extra calcium may help carry oxalates out of the body, leaving less of either for stone formation. Oxalate-containing foods usually contribute only 10 percent of the total oxalate in your body. The rest comes from the breakdown of the amino acid glycine and vitamin C (only megadoses of C are problematic, however).

POSSIBLE STONE FORMERS

People prone to forming calcium-oxalate stones may be asked by their doctor to cut back on the following foods if their urine contains an excess of oxalate:

Beets
Chocolate
Coffee
Cola
Nuts
Rhubarb
Spinach
Strawberries
Tea
Wheat bran

But don't completely avoid these foods without first talking to your doctor. In most cases, these foods can be eaten in limited amounts.

So, what's the bottom line? If you're prone to kidney stones, whether or not you get them is most influenced by how much *oxalate* is present in your urinary tract, not by how much *calcium* is there. You can best prevent kidney stones by getting plenty of calcium in your diet, not overdoing the protein, and, most importantly, drinking lots of fluids to flush potential problems away.

Singular Stones

Uric-acid stones are another, less common type of kidney stone. As you might have guessed, they contain uric acid. That's a substance that forms when purines in protein foods are broken down. When your urine is acidic, these stones are more likely to form. Acidic urine is a problem for people who have a disease called gout.

Not surprisingly, people with gout are more likely than other people to develop uric-acid kidney stones. If you suffer from these stones, you may need to cut back on protein, particularly foods high in purine (see Packed with Purines, below). Your doctor may also prescribe medications to reduce the acidity of your urine.

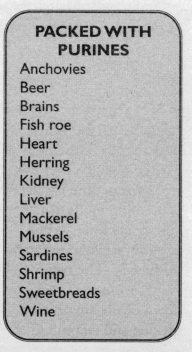

PACKED WITH PURINES

Anchovies
Beer
Brains
Fish roe
Heart
Herring
Kidney
Liver
Mackerel
Mussels
Sardines
Shrimp
Sweetbreads
Wine

LACTOSE INTOLERANCE

✖ ✖ ✖

Milk is often called the perfect food. But nearly 50 million American adults would beg to differ. They suffer from lactose intolerance, and for them, drinking milk or eating dairy products triggers gas, bloating, and cramping.

Lactose is the sugar in milk, and an enzyme called lactase is normally responsible for breaking down lactose in your digestive tract after you've consumed milk or a food made from it. Some people, however, don't make enough lactase enzyme to tackle the lactose they consume. They may be missing a little or a lot of the enzyme. Depending on the degree of enzyme deficiency, consuming dairy products, such as ice cream or cottage cheese, can trigger bouts of nausea, cramps, bloating, gas, or diarrhea, usually 30 minutes or so later.

Lactose Lowdown

What's your nationality or ethnic heritage? It's a good clue to whether you are lactase deficient. Some 90 percent of Asians, for example, suffer some degree of lactose intolerance. As many as 75 percent of all African American, Jewish, Native American, and Mexican American adults are lactose intolerant. In fact, the only population left relatively unscathed by the condition are people of Northern European descent.

But lactose intolerance is not an all-or-nothing

proposition. It's normal for the level of lactase in the intestinal tract to begin declining after three years of age. How steep that decline is varies greatly among individuals, accounting for a spectrum of symptoms ranging from none to a lot of diarrhea, cramping, and gas. The severity of symptoms depends on just how low your levels of the critical enzyme are. In rare cases, children are born without the ability to produce lactase. For most people, though, lactase deficiency is a condition that develops naturally over time. Many people may not experience symptoms until later in life.

Any illness that affects the lactase-producing cells of the small intestine, such as an inflammation of the bowel or even the flu, can trigger a temporary lactase deficiency. In these cases, the condition, referred to as secondary lactase deficiency, is usually temporary; once the illness is over and the damaged cells recover, they begin producing the enzyme again. However, if you have stomach or intestinal surgery, your inability to produce lactase may be permanent.

The variability of symptoms from person to person is so great that one person with lactose intolerance may be able to drink a glass of milk with no symptoms, while someone else with a more severe deficiency might not be able to tolerate a spoonful of milk in coffee without feeling the effects. And the person who had no symptoms from a single glass of milk could invite trouble if they also have ice cream for dessert, thus exceeding their ability to handle lactose.

Intolerance vs. Allergy

One of the most common misconceptions about lactose intolerance is that it is a milk allergy. Though the two are often confused, the difference is a critical one. The inability to completely digest lactose rarely translates into the need for a milk-free diet. But if you have a milk allergy, even minute amounts can trigger a serious reaction. Symptoms of a true milk allergy include a runny nose, puffy eyes, skin rash, vomiting, tightness in the throat, and difficulty breathing. There is no connection between having a milk allergy, which is due to an immune response to a protein, and having lactose intolerance, which is an enzyme deficiency.

Lactose intolerance is most common in adults, whereas milk allergies are seen mostly in children. Essentially all children who develop a milk allergy develop it in their first year or so, and the vast majority will eventually outgrow it. In the end, very few people carry milk allergies with them into late childhood or adulthood.

Living with Lactose

Milk and other dairy products are a major source of nutrients in the diet. An important one that we generally turn to dairy foods to provide is calcium. So, if you cut back on foods high in lactose, you may not meet your needs for calcium and other nutrients.

Fortunately, most people who are lactose deficient don't have to completely cut dairy foods from their diets. In fact, it's been estimated that about 80 percent of people with lactose intolerance are still able to drink enough milk for good nutrition. Many people can drink a cup of milk with a meal without any problems. Drinking milk with other foods slows its digestion and allows the body more time to digest the lactose. Recent research shows that regular intake of lactose may even improve tolerance over time.

Another way to get plenty of bone-building calcium and other nutrients is with lactose-reduced milk, available in the milk case at most groceries. Or you can try lactase-enzyme supplements. Available as over-the-counter caplets or chewable tablets, these supplements are taken along with dairy food. Also available are lactase-enzyme drops that you add to regular milk to predigest the milk's lactose before you drink it (keep in mind, however, that you must add the drops 24 hours in advance of drinking the milk to give the drops time to work).

Just how diligent you must be in avoiding lactose depends entirely on how sensitive you are. But here are a few tips that may help you minimize your lactose problems.

• Give yogurt a try. Many people who suffer lactose intolerance are better able to tolerate yogurt. Yogurts labeled as containing "live active cultures" contain friendly bacteria that help digest lactose. Yogurt is also a good source of calcium.

• Drink chocolate milk. The calcium in chocolate milk is just as well absorbed as that in regular milk, and you may tolerate flavored milk better than plain.

• You may be better able to tolerate aged hard cheeses such as cheddar, Colby, Swiss, and Parmesan. These cheeses contain little lactose compared with milk and softer cheeses because the whey, which contains most of the lactose, separates from the cheese during processing.

• Try drinking milk with your meals, instead of on its own, and drink smaller amounts of milk throughout the day. If you can't tolerate a whole cup of milk at one sitting, you might do just fine having a half cup with your breakfast and another half cup with your evening meal.

• Be aware that lactose is also found in some prescription medications and over-the-counter drugs as an "inactive ingredient." Check labels and/or consult your pharmacist. If there are other suitable medications available that don't contain lactose fillers, you may want to consider switching, but you'll need to discuss this possibility with your doctor first, especially for prescription medications or any nonprescription drugs you need to take on a regular basis.

• Some nondairy foods that may contain lactose include breads, frozen vegetables, soups, salad dressings, cereals, breakfast drinks, cake mixes, and candies. Scan the ingredient lists of these types of products for milk, milk solids, whey, curds, and cheese as clues that lactose is lurking in them.

• Treat buttermilk and acidophilus milk the same as regular milk. They contain lactose, and contrary to what you may have heard before, they are generally no better tolerated than regular milk.

• Fat slows the passage of lactose through your digestive system, giving your body more time to work on digesting it. So if you have trouble tolerating skim milk but don't want all the fat and calories from whole milk, try drinking one percent or two percent milk instead.

OSTEOPOROSIS

✖ ✖ ✖

If ever there was a disease that fits the old saying, "An ounce of prevention is worth a pound of cure," it's osteoporosis. For years, it was thought that calcium was important only for kids. Once you were grown, your bones were built and that was that, right? Wrong.

Osteoporosis is a condition of progressive bone loss that causes bones to become fragile and fracture easily. It is painful, disfiguring, and debilitating. Ten million Americans have osteoporosis, and another 18 million have low bone mass, placing them at risk for this bone-thinning disease.

Osteoporosis usually becomes detectable once you reach your sixties and seventies. We even have a stereotypical "little old lady" image that reflects the changes that can occur with osteoporosis: She's a frail little thing. She's lost several inches of height, because as bone has been lost, her spine has simply begun to collapse. And she's developed a "dowager's hump" that gives her a stooped appearance and causes her frequent back pain. But that image does not actually depict the *typical* woman who has osteoporosis. Usually, the first sign of osteoporosis is a fracture that occurs in a weakened bone. A sudden bump or strain may be all it takes to cause a fracture. If bone loss is severe, something as simple as opening a window can

WHO'S AT RISK?

Here's a list of osteoporosis risk factors. See if you're in line for bone loss.

Female. Women are several times more likely to develop osteoporosis than are men.

Race. Caucasians are at greater risk for developing osteoporosis than darker-skinned people are. Far fewer black women develop osteoporosis than do whites. People of Asian descent are also at higher risk for osteoporosis.

Bone structure. Small or petite women are at greater risk because of their small bones. If they experience the same rate of bone loss as larger women, they will develop osteoporosis sooner, simply because they have less bone to start with.

Early menopause. The earlier a woman experiences menopause, the greater her risk of osteoporosis. Risk also increases if a woman has a surgical menopause—a hysterectomy, or removal of the uterus, or a double oophorectomy, or removal of both ovaries—at an early age and is not put on hormone replacement therapy. If only the uterus is removed but the ovaries are left intact, the woman will likely experience normal menopausal symptoms in her early 50s, on average, and her risk will not be increased.

Family history. Many women with osteoporosis have at least one family member who has the disease. Still, a lack of family history doesn't rule out the possibility that a woman will develop osteoporosis.

Long-term use of certain medications. People suffering from asthma or rheumatoid arthritis who take cortisone (a steroid) for long periods may diminish the strength of their bones.

cause a fragile arm bone to break. Yet until such a fracture occurs, neither the woman nor anyone simply looking at her would likely suspect she has osteoporosis.

Some 45 percent of your bone mass is laid down during your teen years. But, bone density begins to decrease once you're about 35. After menopause, the drop in a woman's bone mass is dramatic. By age 65, the average woman has only about 74 percent of her peak bone mass. A 65-year-old man, on the other hand, still has about 91 percent of his peak bone mass (men also have greater bone mass to begin with). Why do you often hear of older people who break their hips? It's a common clue to osteoporosis, as are the minor bone breaks in the spine that cause loss of height. More than a million people in the United States suffer bone fractures due to osteoporosis each year. Many of those with hip fractures die within a year.

Steps for Prevention

There's no cure for osteoporosis, so the best line of defense is prevention. If you wait until later in life to worry about getting osteoporosis, it's probably too late to completely reverse the damage. But there are steps that can be taken to prevent further bone loss. The National Osteoporosis Foundation recommends:

• Eating a balanced diet rich in calcium and vitamin D
• Engaging in regular weight-bearing exercise

• Maintaining a healthy lifestyle with no smoking or excessive use of alcohol
• Getting your bone density tested, and taking medication when appropriate

Promising research has shown that you can not only slow the progression of osteoporosis, you may even be able to reverse some of the damage. Several studies have shown that postmenopausal women who get adequate calcium can cut bone loss more than 40 percent. And further research has shown that postmenopausal women can actually lay down new

BOOST YOUR CALCIUM INTAKE

• To get extra calcium, use milk in place of water in recipes and mixes, such as oatmeal, pancakes or waffles, cream-style soups, muffins, rice, instant mashed potatoes, and coffee drinks.
• Use plain or flavored yogurt in recipes or as a dressing for fruit salads.
• Make fruit smoothies with yogurt, milk, and fresh or frozen fruit pieces.
• Sprinkle low-fat cheese on vegetables and salads.
• When you make salads, use deep-green lettuce varieties, such as romaine and kale, rather than plain old iceberg. They are richer in calcium.
• Try adding powdered milk to foods such as coffee, tea, soups, casseroles, and batters for bread, cake, cookies, or muffins. Try about ¼ cup per recipe.

MILK-FREE CALCIUM SOURCES

Almonds
Bok choy
Broccoli
Figs
Greens (beet, collard, mustard, turnip)
Herring
Kale
Orange juice, calcium-fortified
Salmon, with bones
Sardines, with bones
Soybeans
Tofu, if it's made with calcium sulfate

bone if they also take estrogen and exercise along with getting enough calcium.

The Dietary Reference Intake (DRI) for calcium, the amount that you should get each day, is 1,000 milligrams for adults 19 to 50 years old. After age 50, the daily need for calcium increases to 1,200 milligrams. During the teen years, calcium requirements are highest, at 1,300 milligrams daily.

For people who don't like milk or other dairy products, there are a few fairly good nondairy food sources of calcium (see Milk-Free Calcium Sources, above). If you are concerned about fat and calories, a wide variety of fat-free and low-fat dairy products are available today to provide you with the calcium you need. Finally, if lactose intolerance is holding you back from enjoying enough milk and dairy products to get the calcium you require, see the Lactose Intolerance profile, page 113, for creative ways to get around your digestive difficulties and indulge in enough dairy to meet your needs.

BONE BUILDERS

Though calcium leads the pack of bone-building nutrients, there are other members of the group that play smaller but equally critical roles in building and maintaining bone.

Phosphorus. Second only to calcium, phosphorus is a major component of bones. In fact, calcium and phosphorus are "codependent"—your body needs both in the right balance to maintain healthy bones. Rich sources include milk and milk products, meat, legumes, nuts, oatmeal, asparagus, and spinach.

Magnesium. This mineral is required for bone formation, although its exact role isn't completely understood. Some studies looking at bone health have found that the more magnesium people consume in their diet, the denser their bones. Good sources of magnesium include bananas, chocolate, nuts, seeds, soybeans, buckwheat, and beans.

Vitamin D. Without enough vitamin D, your body can't take full advantage of the calcium in your diet. You can get plenty of vitamin D from fortified milk or by spending 5 to 15 minutes in the sun two or three times a week. Your skin has the ability to manufacture vitamin D when exposed to ultraviolet rays (unless you're wearing sunscreen).

BONE PROTECTORS

In addition to a diet filled with plenty of bone-building nutrients, there are several lifestyle factors that appear to help lower a woman's risk of developing osteoporosis.

Exercise. Regular weight-bearing exercise is crucial for the development and maintenance of healthy bone tissue. This is true for everyone, from young children to post-menopausal women. What's essential is that the activity you choose be weight-bearing—in other words, your bones and muscles have to support the weight of your body as you perform the activity. Walking is a good example of a weight-bearing exercise, one that most people can do. Swimming, on the other hand, is good exercise for your heart, but it isn't weight bearing (the water supports your body's weight) and it won't keep your bones strong.

The intensity of the exercise doesn't matter in terms of building and maintaining bone, which is good news for those of us who haven't exercised regularly in a while. In fact, you're probably better off with a more moderate pace that you can keep up for a longer period of time, so that you're actually making your bones and muscles bear your weight longer. If you have been relatively sedentary lately or have any chronic health conditions, you should definitely start out slowly and gradually increase your time, pace, and frequency. You should also get your doctor's approval before beginning any new exercise program.

Be sure you wear a pair of comfortable, supportive shoes that fit your feet well, too.

Estrogen replacement therapy. After a woman experiences menopause, estrogen therapy can help forestall bone loss. The amount of estrogen required to both prevent bone loss and alleviate the symptoms of menopause is small, actually less than that in a typical birth control pill. Still, there are risks and possible side effects. So be sure to thoroughly discuss the pros and cons of estrogen replacement with your doctor.

Overweight. This may be one of the few conditions where being overweight actually offers some protection. It's not known exactly why. It could be because the extra weight strengthens bone, or it could be that overweight women produce more estrogen than slender women. Considering the potential negative health effects that are associated with being overweight, such as the increased risks of high blood pressure and diabetes, it is not recommended that you purposely gain excess weight or stay overweight to prevent osteoporosis. However, it certainly highlights one of the many potential negative side effects of the waif-like, model-thin figure that is often glorified in the fashion industry and that is generally attainable only through disordered, unhealthy eating behaviors.

Pregnancy. Your risk of developing osteoporosis is greater if you have never been pregnant. Though being pregnant lowers your risk, it's not known if multiple pregnancies lower your risk further or whether, in fact, they might actually increase it.

THE CALCIUM ROBBERS

There are also bone robbers—some you might never suspect—that you'll want to avoid or limit for the health of your bones.

Alcohol. It's been suggested that small amounts of alcohol, say three to six drinks per week, may actually help your body to retain calcium and prevent osteoporosis by raising estrogen levels. But too much alcohol clearly weakens bones and damages your overall health. And the flip side to the estrogen coin is that the higher estrogen levels that are associated with moderate alcohol intake may be linked to an increased risk for breast cancer. So if you imbibe at all, go easy.

Caffeine. Excessive caffeine intake, whether from coffee or other caffeinated drinks, can cause your body to lose calcium, but the effects are not quite as extreme as once thought. The amount of caffeine in a cup of coffee cancels the calcium in only about one tablespoon of milk. Still, it's probably a good idea to keep your daily caffeine intake to no more than about three cups of brewed coffee or four cups of brewed tea. Keep in mind that other food products, including caffeinated soft drinks, can add to your caffeine intake.

Inactivity. It has been proven beyond a doubt that regular physical activity is absolutely crucial to maintaining bone health throughout your life, so being sedentary means you're missing a simple, inexpensive, low-risk way to prevent calcium from leaching out of your bones—perhaps the simplest way to keep your bones healthy and strong. Indeed, it's like letting calcium simply slip through your fingers.

Protein. In the United States, we generally eat far more protein than we need for good health. And it's believed that a high protein intake causes calcium to be excreted. Over time, this calcium loss, if not compensated for with dietary calcium, will come from the bones.

Smoking. Women who smoke tend to reach menopause earlier than nonsmokers, and this may be what increases their risk for osteoporosis. Smoking may also encourage bone loss in other ways that have yet to be identified. Ask your doctor for help in quitting.

Uncovering Osteoporosis

If you are going through menopause, get your bone density tested with absorptiometry. This special type of X-ray is necessary because regular X-rays can detect bone loss only after you've already lost at least 25 percent of your bone mass. The results of the test will help you and your doctor decide if estrogen replacement therapy or another type of medication is right for you.

PART II

✖ ✖ ✖

PRESERVING FOOD'S HEALING POWER

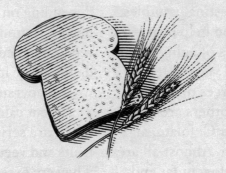

FRUITS AND VEGETABLES

✕ ✕ ✕

You've heard it before—and you'll hear it again: Eat your fruits and vegetables! There is no doubt that a diet with plenty of fruits and vegetables offers a whole host of health benefits, including protection from heart disease, stroke, high blood pressure, some types of cancer, eye disease, and gastrointestinal troubles. It can even help beat back the effects of aging. Some fruits and vegetables are good sources of vitamin A, while others are rich in vitamin C, folate, and potassium. Almost all are naturally low in fat and calories, none have cholesterol, and many are great sources of fiber. Fruits and vegetables also add wonderful flavors, textures, and colors to your diet.

Pick More Produce

The latest MyPyramid guidelines recommend a daily intake of 2 cups of fruit and 2½ cups of vegetables for a person eating a 2,000 calorie-a-day diet. Higher or lower amounts are recommended, depending on your caloric needs. To find the amount recommended for your daily caloric intake, visit www.mypyramid.gov.

To cut calories and fat, take extra servings of fruits and vegetables. They are excellent and satisfying substitutes for higher-calorie meats and sweets. Here's what counts as a one-cup serving:

Fruits
- 1 medium piece of fruit
- 1 cup cut-up or cooked fruit
- 1 large banana
- ¼ small cantaloupe
- ½ cup dried fruit
- 1 cup berries or grapes
- 1 cup 100% fruit juice

Vegetables
- 1 cup raw or cooked vegetables
- 2 cups raw leafy vegetables
- 1 cup baby carrots (approximately 12 carrots)
- 1 medium potato
- 1 cup cooked or canned dried beans or peas
- 1 cup vegetable juice

Eat a Rainbow

If you haven't been eating much in the way of produce, choosing any kind of fruit or vegetable more often is a great start. But to get the biggest bang for your bite, think in color. Choosing assorted colors of fruits and vegetables is a great strategy for making sure you get the most nutritional value from your produce choices. In fact, an eating plan centered around colorful fruits and vegetables receives hearty endorsement from the National Cancer Institute, the American Cancer Society, and the Produce for Better Health Foundation.

In many cases, the deeper and darker the color of the fruit or vegetable, the greater the amount of nutrients it contains. For example, spinach offers eight times more vitamin C than does iceberg lettuce, and a ruby red grapefruit offers 25 times more vitamin A than a white grapefruit. Yet every fruit and vegetable has a unique complement of vitamins, minerals, fiber, and phytonutrients that provide benefits. So it's important to sample from the complete color spectrum as well as to eat a variety within each color group. Here are some ideas to expand your produce palette.

BLUE/PURPLE

These fruits and vegetables contain varying amounts of health-promoting phytonutrients, such as polyphenols and anthocyanins. The pigments that give these foods their rich color pack a powerful antioxidant punch (see the antioxidant discussion in the Cancer profile, page 21). Blue and purple produce give you extra protection against some types of cancer and urinary tract infections, plus they may help boost brain health and vision.

Fruits
Blackberries
Blueberries
Currants, black
Elderberries
Figs, purple
Grapes, purple
Plums
Prunes
Raisins

Vegetables
Asparagus, purple
Belgian endive, purple
Cabbage, purple
Carrots, purple
Eggplant
Peppers, purple
Potatoes, purple-fleshed

GREEN

Green fruits and vegetables contain varying amounts of potent phytochemicals, such as lutein and indoles, as well as other essential nutrients. These substances can help lower cancer risk, improve eye health, and keep bones and teeth strong.

Fruits
Apples, green
Avocados
Grapes, green
Honeydew
Kiwifruit
Limes
Pears, green

Vegetables
Artichokes
Arugula
Asparagus
Beans, green
Broccoflower
Broccoli
Broccoli rabe
Brussels sprouts
Cabbage, Chinese
Cabbage, green
Celery
Chayote squash
Cucumbers
Endive
Greens, leafy
Leeks
Lettuce
Okra
Onions, green
Peas, green (or English)
Peas, snow
Peas, sugar snap
Peppers, green
Spinach
Watercress
Zucchini

WHITE/TAN/BROWN
White, tan, and brown fruits and vegetables contain varying amounts of phytonutrients, such as allicin, found in the onion family. These fruits and vegetables play a role in heart health by helping you maintain healthy cholesterol levels, and they may lower the risk of some types of cancer.

Fruits
Bananas
Dates

Nectarines, white
Peaches, white
Pears, brown

Vegetables
Cauliflower
Corn, white
Garlic
Ginger
Jerusalem artichoke
Jicama
Kohlrabi
Mushrooms
Onions
Parsnips
Potatoes, white-fleshed
Shallots
Turnips

YELLOW/ORANGE

Orange and yellow fruits
and vegetables contain
varying amounts of
antioxidants, such as
vitamin C, as well as other
phytonutrients, including
carotenoids and biofla-
vonoids. These substances
may help promote heart
and vision health and a
healthy immune system;
they may also help to ward
off cancer.

Fruits
Apples, yellow
Apricots
Cantaloupe
Cape gooseberries
Figs, yellow
Grapefruit
Kiwifruit, golden
Lemons
Mangoes
Nectarines
Oranges
Papaya
Peaches
Pears, yellow
Persimmons
Pineapple
Tangerines
Watermelon, yellow

Vegetables
Beets, yellow
Carrots
Corn, sweet
Peppers, yellow
Potatoes, yellow
Pumpkin

Rutabagas
Squash, butternut
Squash, yellow summer
Squash, yellow winter
Sweet potatoes
Tomatoes, yellow

RED

Phytonutrients in red produce that have health-promoting properties include lycopene, ellagic acid, and anthocyanins. Red fruits and vegetables may help maintain heart health, memory function, and urinary tract health as well as lower the risk of some types of cancer.

Fruits
Apples, red
Cherries
Cranberries
Grapefruit, pink/red
Grapes, red
Oranges, blood
Pears, red
Pomegranates
Raspberries

Strawberries
Watermelon

Vegetables
Beets
Onions, red
Peppers, red
Potatoes, red
Radicchio
Radishes
Rhubarb
Tomatoes

Fresh and Beyond

There are lots of easy, nutritious, and affordable ways to enjoy fruits and vegetables all year long:

• Buy in season. Some types of fresh produce are great buys year-round, such as bananas, apples, broccoli, potatoes, carrots, cabbage, and spinach. Other items are more affordable—and better tasting—at certain times of the year. If your community offers a farmer's market, be sure to frequent it for extra-fresh produce.

• Go for convenience. Try prewashed and/or precut salad greens, baby carrots, and chopped fresh vegetables. The time savings can be huge, and the waste very little.

• Can it. Canned goods can be a low-cost, convenient way to enjoy your fruits and vegetables. Canned fruits and vegetables are generally comparable in vitamins and fiber to their fresh and frozen counterparts. Look for fruits packed in juice or water. Wash away extra sugar from canned fruits and extra salt from canned vegetables by rinsing them under cold water after opening.

• Hit the sales. Look for great deals offered by your local grocery store. Often, bargain prices on fruits and vegetables are used to draw in customers. Check the food ads before you shop. Since you're looking for variety, try the items that are on sale, even if some are new to you.

• Join the cold rush. Flash-freezing fruits and vegetables keeps all the important nutrients locked in tight. Frozen produce is handy to keep in your freezer for whenever you need it. Look for mixtures of vegetables to use in soups or stir-frys or to just steam or microwave and eat. Look for fruits frozen without added sugar.

Is It Ripe Yet?

When shopping for fresh fruits, you'll want to consider ripeness. As fruit ripens, the starch turns to sugar, which gives fruits their characteristic sweet taste. Some fruits continue to ripen after they're harvested, while others do not. Whether or not a fruit continues to ripen determines its storage and shelf life. For fruits that continue to ripen, it's a good idea to select them at varying stages of ripeness so they're not all ripe at the same time.

Fruits that require additional ripening should be stored at room temperature until they reach the desired ripeness. To hasten the ripening of some fruits, such as pears and peaches, put them in a loosely closed paper bag on the counter. They'll be ready to eat in a day or two. If fruits become overly ripe, instead of tossing them, try trimming any blemishes, then cooking and puréeing the fruit to make sauces for dressings or desserts. Fruits that do not ripen after harvesting should be stored in a cool area, such as the refrigerator, until you are ready to eat them.

Fruits that will continue to ripen:

Apricots
Avocados
Bananas
Cantaloupe
Kiwi
Nectarines
Peaches
Pears
Plums
Tomatoes

Fruits to buy ripe and ready to eat:

Apples
Cherries
Grapefruit
Grapes
Lemons

Limes
Oranges
Pineapple
Strawberries
Tangerines
Watermelon

prepare them that will determine how nutritious they are when you eat them.

Keeping Your Produce Nutritious

Fruits and vegetables are naturally nutritious. It's how you store, clean, and

STORAGE

Fresh, properly stored produce will be the most nutritious. To keep produce fresh longer, store it

---

MAXIMIZE THE FIBER

Did you know the fiber content of different forms of the same food can vary considerably?

• Raw apple with skin: 3.5 grams of fiber

• ½ cup applesauce: 1.5 grams of fiber

• ¾ cup apple juice: little or no fiber

In the above example, the skin offers much of the fiber. Here's another example with a different slant.

• 1 cup raw spinach: about 1 gram of fiber

• 1 cup cooked spinach: about 3 grams of fiber

In this case, the spinach cooks down so you're eating a larger amount of the raw equivalent and thus getting more fiber.

---

unwashed and uncut. With the exception of a few items, such as garlic, onions, potatoes, and winter squash, fresh produce should be stored in the refrigerator. Most produce items are best stored loose in crisper drawers, which have a slightly higher humidity. If your refrigerator doesn't have a crisper drawer, use moisture-resistant wrap or bags to hold your produce. Fruits and vegetables that have already been cut and/or washed should be covered tightly to prevent vitamin loss and stored on refrigerator shelves.

CLEANING

Wash your produce in clean water. This important step should be done for all fruits and vegetables, even for produce such as melons and oranges that have skin or rinds that you don't plan to eat. That's because surface dirt or bacteria can contaminate your produce when you cut or peel it.

Plan to wash your produce just before you're ready to eat or cook it to reduce spoilage caused by excess moisture. The one exception is lettuce—it remains crisp when you wash and refrigerate it for later use. It is not advisable to use detergent when washing fruits and vegetables. Produce is porous and can absorb the detergent, which leaves a soapy residue. Special produce rinses or sprays can help loosen surface dirt and waxes.

Clean thicker-skinned vegetables and fruits with a soft-bristled brush. Peel and discard outer leaves or rinds. If you plan to eat the nutrient-rich skin of hearty vegetables, such as potatoes and carrots, scrub the skin well with a soft-bristled brush. For cleaning fragile berries, such as strawberries, raspberries, blackberries, and blueberries, the best method is to spray them with the kitchen-sink sprayer. Use a colander so dirt and water can drain, and gently turn the fruit as you spray.

PREPARATION

There are plenty of ways to enjoy fruits and vegetables. Eat them raw whenever possible to get maximum nutrition. For vegetables that require cooking, such as asparagus, green beans, or brussels sprouts, cook as quickly as possible—just until tender crisp. This helps to minimize loss of nutrients and also helps vegetables retain their bright color and flavor.

Cook vegetables (and fruits) in a covered pot with just a little water—to help create steam that speeds cooking. Or try cooking in the microwave. This fast method of cooking helps to retain nutrients, flavor, and crispness.

Easy Ways to Get Your Helpings

• Start your day with fruit—add fresh or dried fruit to cereal, yogurt, pancakes, or waffles, or just enjoy it by itself.

• Mix chopped vegetables into scrambled eggs, or fold them into an omelet.

• First, freeze fresh fruits, such as grapes, blueberries, and chunks of bananas, peaches, or mango. Then, enjoy them as a refreshing snack, or mix them with yogurt and juice in a blender to make a smoothie.

• Snack on a trail mix of crunchy, whole-grain cereal, dried fruits, and chopped, toasted almonds.

• Bring a prepackaged fruit cup, box of raisins, or piece of fruit with you to work or school for an energy-boosting snack.

• For a short-cut fruit salad, open two or more cans of chopped or sliced fruit and add some fresh or frozen fruits for a tasty and refreshing snack or meal accompaniment.

• Stuff a pita pocket with veggie chunks and sprouts, and drizzle on a low-fat ranch dressing.

• Toss pasta or rice with leftover vegetables, low-fat vinaigrette, and a sprinkling of shredded cheese or toasted pine nuts or almonds.

• Sneak in some extra helpings of produce by adding finely chopped vegetables, such as carrots, eggplant, broccoli, or cauliflower, to marinara sauce, soups, stews, and chili.

• Roast your vegetables for a deep, rich flavor. Drizzle them with a little olive oil, and roast in an oven set to 425 degrees Fahrenheit or on the grill until tender. Try carrots, asparagus, butternut squash, eggplant, broc-coli—or just about any vegetable that strikes your fancy!

BREADS, CEREALS, RICE, AND PASTA

This group of foods has one thing in common—they are all made from grains. Any food made from wheat, rice, oats, corn, or another cereal is a grain product. These foods should form the foundation of the diet for several reasons. First, grain-based foods are rich in complex carbohydrates, your body's best energy source. As the body's key fuel, carbohydrates provide your brain, heart, and nervous system with a constant supply of energy to keep you moving, breathing, and thinking.

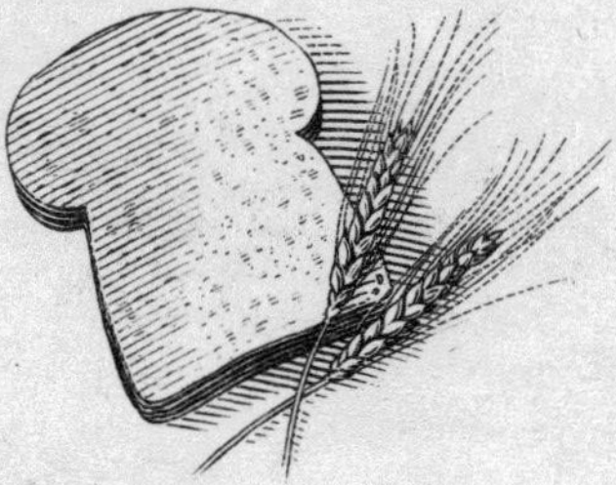

Grain products also supply B vitamins and iron (especially if they're enriched or include the whole grain), as well as other beneficial phytonutrients (substances in plants with health-protective effects). In addition, many grain-based foods supply fiber.

The "Whole" Story

An important strategy for choosing the best grain foods is to seek out products made from *whole* grains. A whole grain is the entire edible part of any grain, whether it's wheat, oats, corn, rice, or a more exotic grain. The three layers of a grain kernel each supply important nutrients:

• The outer protective coating, or bran, is packed with fiber, B vitamins, protein, and trace minerals.

• The endosperm supplies mostly carbohydrate and protein and some B vitamins.

• The germ is rich in B vitamins, vitamin E, trace minerals, antioxidants, and phytonutrients.

When whole grains are milled (refined), the bran and the germ portions are removed, leaving only the endosperm. Unfortunately, more than half the fiber and almost three-quarters of the vitamins and minerals are in the bran and germ. When you eat foods made from whole grains, you get the nutritional benefits of the entire grain.

Enriched grain products add back some of the B vitamins—thiamin, folic acid, riboflavin, and niacin—and iron lost when the grain was milled. But lots of other nutrients and fiber don't get added back.

Whole-Grain Goodness

The individual nutrients in whole-grain foods— fiber, antioxidants (see the Cancer profile, page 21, for a discussion of antioxidants), phytonutrients, and vitamins and minerals—each offer important health benefits of their own. When they work together in the "whole" food, however, they interact in powerful ways that help protect your health. For example, a diet rich in whole-grain foods is associated with lower risk for several chronic diseases and conditions including heart disease, cancer, diabetes, and gastrointestinal troubles. It can also play a role in the treatment of many of these diseases.

A wide array of whole-grain foods is available in today's supermarkets. Examples of foods that can be found in whole-grain versions include breads, ready-to-eat and hot cereals, brown rice, pasta, crackers, tortillas, pancakes, waffles, and muffins. You just need to know what to look for (see Get Your Whole Grain's Worth on the next page).

Your Daily Grains

The latest MyPyramid guidelines recommend eating three or more ounces of whole-grain foods each day. At least half of your grain choices should come from whole grains. To find the total amount of grains you should be eating, visit www.mypyramid.gov.

A one-ounce serving of a grain food is equivalent to any of these:

• 1 slice bread

• 1 ounce (about 1 cup) ready-to-eat cereal

• ½ bagel, English muffin, or bun

• ½ cup cooked cereal, rice, or pasta

• 1 four-inch-diameter pancake or waffle

• 1 seven-inch-diameter tortilla

• 5–6 whole-grain crackers

• 3 cups popcorn

Be sure to figure how many "ounce-equivalents" are in the portions you eat. You'll probably be surprised at how quickly grains add up.

Get Your Whole Grain's Worth

When you're choosing among grain products, follow these tips to get the most fiber- and nutrient-filled forms.

Breakfast cereals:
• Look for "whole grain" on the front of the package.
• The words "whole grain" or "whole" appear in front of wheat, oats, rice, corn, barley, or another grain as the first ingredient. Hint: Oats are always whole, even if they're rolled, instant, fine-cut, or coarse-cut.

Breads, tortillas, and crackers:
• Look for "whole wheat" or "whole grain" in the product's name.

• A whole-grain flour, such as whole-wheat flour, should be the first ingredient listed. Wheat flour, enriched flour, and degerminated cornmeal are *not* whole grain.

WHOLE-GRAIN CUES

You may see a "whole grain" seal or emblem on a grain-food package—some manufacturers have created their own seal to signify that a product is made from whole grains. Or you may see this FDA-authorized health claim: *"Diets rich in whole-grain foods and other plant foods that are low in total fat, saturated fat, and cholesterol, may reduce the risk of heart disease and certain cancers."* Foods that bear this claim must contain at least 51 percent or more whole grains by weight and be low in fat.

Pasta and rice:

• Only brown rice is whole grain.

• Look for pasta made from whole-wheat flour. Hint: Some pastas are made with a mix of whole-wheat and white flours; they may be a good stepping stone or compromise if you're having trouble adjusting to the texture of whole-wheat-only pastas.

Your Daily Bread and More

Try some of these easy ways to make grains—especially whole grains—a regular part of your day.

• Get the first of your three ounces of whole grains from a whole-grain breakfast cereal.

• Use whole-wheat pasta in hearty soups, hot casseroles, and chilled salads.

• Make the switch to brown rice, or try a combination of brown and white rice.

• When you make bread, muffins, biscuits, cookies, pancakes, or waffles, substitute whole-wheat flour for half of the white flour, or add some oats, wheat germ, or bran cereal.

• Take a whole grain to lunch—a sandwich on whole-grain bread is one way to go, or add some new appeal to your lunchtime meal with a whole-grain bagel, roll, tortilla, or pita.

• Snack on popcorn, low-fat granola made with whole oats, brown-rice cakes, or snack mixes made with whole-grain cereal.

• Sprinkle wheat germ, oat bran, or bran cereal on yogurt, salads, or cut-up fruit. Or use it to coat fish

TALES AND TRUTHS ABOUT GRAINS

Tale: Stone-ground, 100 percent wheat, cracked wheat, multigrain, pumpernickel, and bran are other names for whole grain.

Truth: None of these labels on a package guarantees a product is made from whole grains. Check the ingredient list to know for sure. Bran cereals are certainly nutritious, high-fiber options, but they don't include all parts of the grain. And just because a bread's label says it's made from 100 percent wheat flour doesn't mean it's not processed wheat flour, which is nutritionally equivalent to white flour.

Tale: If a bread, cracker, or cereal is dark brown, it's made from whole grains.

Truth: Color does not signal whole grain. Bread is often brown because molasses or caramel coloring has been added. Many whole-oat products, such as oatmeal and oat cereals, are very light in color.

Tale: "Processed" grain foods are not healthy.

Truth: Processed foods such as ready-to-eat cereals and crackers can be excellent sources of nutrients and fiber. Many processed grain foods can still be whole grain as long as all the parts of the grain remain after processing.

Tale: Grain foods are fattening.

Truth: To the contrary, most grain foods are relatively low in calories and naturally low in fat. It's the toppings, sauces, and spreads often added to grain foods that can make them fattening. Some grain-based foods, such as doughnuts, cookies, and pastries, have fat added in preparation. It's wise to go easy on these and balance them with lower-fat and higher-fiber grain choices.

or chicken or to top a tuna casserole. When you prepare a meat loaf or any meat mixture, add some bran cereal or wheat germ instead of bread crumbs.

• Be adventurous and try whole grains you've never tasted, such as whole-grain barley, bulgur, kasha, amaranth, quinoa, and couscous. Note: If you can't find whole-grain barley, choose scotch barley or pot barley, instead of pearled barley, which has lost a greater amount of fiber and nutrients in processing.

Grain Storage

All cereal should be stored in a dry location. Keep the inner bag folded down tightly to keep bugs out, or store the cereal in a container with a tight-fitting lid. Once opened, it'll keep for a few months before it goes stale, unless you live in a humid environment. If so, your best bet is not to buy the large box unless you know you'll finish it in a month or so. Another option is to transfer the cereal to a resealable plastic bag and refrigerate it.

Keep oats in a dark, dry location in a well-sealed container to keep bugs out. Store the container in the refrigerator if you live in a humid locale. The oats will keep up to a year. Whole-oat groats are more likely to become rancid, so be sure to refrigerate them.

Dried pasta is fine stored in your cupboards for months, especially if transferred to airtight containers. Putting your colored pastas in see-through glass jars makes a pretty display, but they'll lose B vitamins that way;

better to keep them cool and dry, away from light, and sealed up tight. Rice and other grains are also best stored in a cool, dark location. Brown rice is more perishable than white rice. It keeps only about six months—slightly longer if you refrigerate it.

Because of its fat content, wheat germ goes rancid easily. Always store opened wheat germ in the refrigerator in a tightly sealed container. If you buy it in a jar, you can simply store it in the refrigerator in its original container. Fresh wheat germ should smell something like toasted nuts, not musty. Unopened, a sealed jar of wheat germ will keep for about one year. Once opened, it can keep up to nine months in the refrigerator if the jar is resealed tightly.

Whole-wheat breads may not have preservatives added. To prevent your bread from going stale, leave out at room temperature only as much as you'll eat in the next day or two, and keep it tightly closed in a plastic bag. Put the rest in the freezer. It defrosts quickly at room temperature if you take out one or two slices as needed. Or you can defrost a few slices in a jiffy in the microwave. But don't refrigerate your bread—it actually goes stale faster.

MEAT, POULTRY, FISH, DRIED BEANS, NUTS, AND SEEDS

✳ ✳ ✳

Foods in this group are diverse, but they have something important in common—protein. The amount and quality of the protein in these foods varies. Animal foods contain high-quality, or complete, protein, which means they supply all the amino acids your body needs to build the protein used to support body functions. Plant sources of protein supply lesser amounts, and except for soybeans, the proteins are not complete. What that means is that a single plant source does not provide all of the amino acids necessary to form complete proteins. You need to consume a variety of plant foods to get all the amino acids needed to form complete proteins.

Besides protein, foods from this group supply varying amounts of other key nutrients, including iron, zinc, magnesium, vitamin E, and B vitamins (thiamin, niacin, and vitamins B_6 and B_{12}). On the downside, some of the foods in this group contain higher amounts of fat, saturated fat, and some cholesterol.

How Much Should You Eat?

The latest MyPyramid guidelines recommend 5½ ounces daily for a 2,000-calorie-a-day diet. Visit www.mypyramid.gov to see how much you need. Any of the following counts as a one-ounce serving from this group:

- 1 ounce cooked lean meat, poultry, or fish
- 1 ounce lean, sliced deli meat (turkey, ham, beef, or bologna)
- 1 ounce canned tuna or salmon, packed in water
- ¼ cup cooked lentils, peas, or dried beans
- 1 egg
- 1 tablespoon peanut butter
- ½ ounce nuts or seeds
- ¼ cup tofu (about 2 ounces)
- 1-ounce soy burger

Lean Red Meat

Could it be that red meat—wonderful, juicy, stick-to-your-ribs red meat—might actually have healing properties, other than the obvious way it makes your taste buds come alive? Why yes, yes it could. But you must honor the word "lean" in front. And you may need to cast meat as a bit player rather than the main character in your meals (sorry, but that means no more eating an entire 16-ounce steak in one sitting). Lean red meat, including beef, veal, and pork (sometimes referred to as "the other white meat"), can indeed be part of a healthful diet. They contribute nutrients that may help you maintain good health and prevent or even fight disease.

Beef, veal, and pork are packed with high-quality protein. They are also a nutrient-dense source of iron and zinc, minerals that many Americans have trouble getting. While it is possible to get enough iron or zinc without eating meat, it's not easy. Eating lean meat is also a dandy way to get vitamin B_{12}, niacin, and vitamin B_6. So, including some lean meat in your diet can be nutritionally uplifting.

The iron in red meat, especially beef, carries a double bonus. About half the iron in beef is heme iron, a highly usable form found only in animal products. And the absorption of the nonheme iron in meat is enhanced by the fact that it's in meat. Eating meat also enhances the absorption of nonheme iron from plant foods. (That's also a good reason to use smaller portions of meat mixed with plant foods in your meals.) The zinc in meat is absorbed better than the zinc in grains and legumes, as well.

And despite the bad press red meat has some-times received, recent research has shown that eating lean beef, veal, and pork is just as effective in lowering bad LDL cho-lesterol and raising good HDL cholesterol in your blood as is eating lean poultry and fish. Plus, close to half the fat in lean beef is monounsaturated, the kind that helps lower blood cholesterol and reduce the risk of heart disease when it replaces saturated fat in the diet. And much of the satu-rated fat that beef does contain is stearic acid, a form that doesn't appear to raise blood cholesterol the way other saturated fats do.

SELECTION AND STORAGE

The secrets to fitting red meat into a healthful eating plan are choosing lean cuts, trimming visible fat, preparing them without adding fat, and eating reasonable portions. When selecting red meat, here are some tips for finding the "skinniest" cuts.

Beef: Look for beef cuts with "loin" or "round" in the name, such as top round, round tip, top sirloin, bottom round, top loin, and tenderloin.

Veal: Lean cuts include cutlet, blade or arm steak, rib roast, and rib or loin chop.

Pork or lamb: Look for cuts with "loin" or "leg" in the name. Pork cuts include tenderloin, top loin roast, top loin chop, center loin chop, sirloin roast, and loin rib chop. Lamb cuts include leg, loin chop, arm chop, and foreshanks.

You can also look for cuts labeled "lean" or "extra lean." According to federal labeling regulations, cuts of meat labeled "lean" must contain ten grams of fat or less per three-ounce serving, and cuts labeled "extra lean" must contain five grams of fat or less per three-ounce serving. Don't be confused by ground beef labeled with a number followed by "percent lean." This refers to the weight of the lean meat versus the fat. For the leanest ground beef, simply look for ground beef that is at least 92 to 95 percent lean—it contains about five grams of total fat per three-ounce serving. Or look for ground round, which is the leanest, followed by ground sirloin, ground chuck, then regular ground beef.

When it comes to portions, forget the 14-ounce steak. To put a reasonable portion in perspective, three ounces of meat is about the size of your palm or a deck of playing cards. If you choose to eat all of your meat group servings at one meal, you can enjoy a steak that weighs about five to seven ounces or is about the size of two decks of cards. Or you can include a smaller portion of meat as a side dish and load up on vegetables and grains instead.

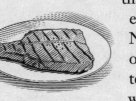

No matter the cut, choose raw meat that looks evenly red (grayish-pink for veal and pork) and not dried out. Refrigerate all meat as soon as you get it home. Place it on a plate so drippings won't contaminate other foods. If you don't plan to cook the meat within three to four days (one to two days for ground meat), freeze it.

PREPARATION AND SERVING TIPS

Defrost meat in the refrigerator, in the microwave, or sitting in cold water that you change every hour. Never let it sit out at room temperature, which invites bacteria to multiply.

Choose your cooking method to match your cut of meat. Some lean cuts, such as beef cuts from the round, do better with a method that includes a liquid, such as braising or stewing. Grilling, roasting, broiling, and pan-frying work well for beef loin cuts. To minimize risk of foodborne illness, be sure ground meat is cooked until the internal temperature is 160 degrees

Fahrenheit—or until the center is no longer pink and juices run clear. Roasts and steaks should be cooked until the internal temperature is at least 145 degrees Fahrenheit. Pork needs to cook to an internal temperature of at least 160 degrees Fahrenheit.

Trim all visible fat from meat before cooking. If you cannot buy ground meat as lean as you like, you can reduce the fat by placing cooked ground meat in a colander and pouring hot water over it. To tenderize tough lean cuts, try marinating, which also adds flavor, or do it the old-fashioned way and pound your meat with a mallet to break down the connective tissue.

Poultry

Chicken and turkey are often considered healthy, low-fat alternatives to beef, but that's not always true. A piece of dark meat, such as a chicken thigh, with the skin on can carry a hefty fat load. You have to make the right poultry choices to really save on fat. Your best bet? Skinless white-meat chicken or turkey. It's lowest in fat and calories. Removing the skin before eating poultry saves fat and calories. But you quickly lose your low-fat advantage if you deep-fry it, smother it in fatty sauces or gravies, or cover it with cheese.

If you're trying to cut back on fat, skinless white-meat poultry offers a great low-fat protein option. You should be aware, however, that chicken and turkey contain about the same amount of cholesterol per serving as beef. Poultry is a generous source of some B vitamins that aren't as plentiful in beef, but it is only a fair source of iron.

Ground turkey is also available, but often it's higher in fat than you might think because it may also contain ground turkey skin. For a truly low-fat ground turkey, look for "ground turkey breast."

SELECTION AND STORAGE

When choosing a whole chicken or turkey, look for one that is plump and firm with skin that looks moist and supple. The skin should have a creamy white or yellowish color (color varies depending on what the bird was fed), and it should have no odor.

Poultry is a highly perishable food that presents a standing invita-tion to bacteria if it's not stored properly. If you buy a fresh, whole chicken or turkey, be sure to store it right away in the coldest part of your refrigerator and use it with-in two to three days. If you don't plan to use it within that time, wash it, dry it, cut it into parts, wrap it, and freeze it. It will keep for up to nine months. If you freeze it whole, it will keep for one year.

Never let poultry thaw at room temperature. Thaw it in the refrigerator, and set it on a plate to catch drippings. It will take anywhere from one to two days to thaw a small 8- to 12-pound turkey, four to five days for a 20-pounder.

RECONSIDERING THE EGG

Eggs were once considered too high in cholesterol and fat to have a place on a heart-healthy menu. Many people still hold to the outdated advice to limit eggs to one or two a week. But unless you're following a very low-fat diet and your doctor insists on it, you can probably safely increase your weekly egg allowance.

Several years ago, scientists discovered that eggs contain less cholesterol than originally thought. This led to the old weekly egg allowance of one to two being upped to three or four eggs. More recently, experts decided that it would be safe to eat up to one whole egg per day.

It turns out that for most people, dietary cholesterol has only a small effect in terms of raising blood cholesterol. Rather, it's saturated fat in the diet that has the greatest effect in causing blood cholesterol levels to rise. In studies where healthy participants ate up to one egg per day, there was no detectable effect on heart disease.

Although recommendations for strict limitations on eating eggs have been dropped, the American Heart Association still recommends keeping cholesterol intake to an average of 300 milligrams per day. One egg contains about 213 milligrams of cholesterol and 5 grams of fat, of which only 1.5 grams are saturated. So an egg a day can fit in a heart-healthy diet if your overall diet is otherwise low in cholesterol.

PREPARATION AND SERVING TIPS

When you handle raw poultry, wash your hands thoroughly afterward with soap and warm water before you touch any other food or utensil. Also be sure to thoroughly wash the cutting board and utensils used during preparation. Skip this important food-safety step and you're risking cross contamination—transferring bacteria like salmonella from raw poultry to other foods served at the meal. Cooking kills salmonella bacteria, but if the bug is transferred to a raw salad, for example, food poisoning can result.

If you marinate chicken or turkey, do it in the refrigerator, not on the kitchen counter at room temperature. And don't use the marinade as a sauce for the cooked bird unless you boil the marinade before serving.

Though fried chicken is an American favorite, especially the fast-food variety, it's also loaded with fat. Opt for lower-fat methods of preparation. Roasting is a good fat-saving cooking technique for whole chickens and turkeys. Skinless chicken or turkey breasts are perfect for marinating in low-fat sauces or, when cut up and mixed with vegetables, for stir-frying. Chicken or turkey breasts also work well on the grill. If you want to add a sauce, wait until the poultry is almost done. Spread it on any sooner and it could scorch and burn before the breast is cooked all the way through.

No matter how you prepare chicken or turkey, be sure it's cooked thoroughly to an internal temperature of 180 degrees Fahrenheit for whole birds and dark meat and to 170 degrees Fahrenheit for boneless roasts and breast meat—the meat should be white, not pink, and the juices should run clear.

Standard advice has long been to remove the skin of chicken or turkey before you cook it to save fat and calories. But it turns out that fat and calories are about the same whether the skin is removed before or after cooking. Since skinless poultry tends to dry out during cooking, keep the skin on while cooking to hold in moisture and flavor. Just remember to remove the skin and any fat left behind before eating.

Fish

Fish makes a fabulous addition to any healthy diet. Its fat content is generally low (many types provide 20 percent or less of calories from fat), making it a great protein option. And the fat it does contain appears to hold promise of preventing and healing disease.

Eating fish instead of meat or poultry usually means less total fat, but it almost always means less saturated fat (as long as you're not ordering a deep-fried fillet and smothering it with tartar sauce). And that's important when it comes to the health of your heart and blood vessels. Ironically, though, fatty fish are better for you than lean fish, because they contain more omega-3 fatty acids.

Two omega-3 fats, eicosapentaenoic acid (EPA) and docosahexaenoic acid (DHA), do a ton of good for your heart. EPA reduces the stickiness of blood platelets, preventing blood clots that can lead to heart attack and stroke. They also reduce triglyceride levels (see Heart Disease and Stroke for a discussion of the importance of triglycerides). DHA helps prevent irregular heartbeats by stabilizing electrical activity in the heart. One study has linked omega-3s with less risk of sudden cardiac death. Another found that older people who eat just one serving of fatty fish a week are 44 percent less likely to die from a heart attack. And more recent research has confirmed the benefits of eating fish for both men and women. The Physician's Health Study of 22,000 men, for example, found that those with the highest blood levels of omega-3s had the least risk of sudden death. And the Nurses' Health Study of 85,000 women found two to four servings a week reduced heart-disease risk by one-third. Even those who ate fish as little as one to three times a month showed benefits. As a result of much of this research, the American Heart Association now recommends two weekly servings of fish. (Supplements of fish oils, on the other hand, are not generally recommended by medical experts because higher doses— which are possible with supplements but improbable through consumption of fish—may cause bleeding problems.)

RISKY FISH?

In contrast to its potential healing properties, fish has been dogged by safety questions. Pesticides, mercury, and chemicals such as PCBs sometimes find their way into fish.

Fattier fish, which is richer in omega-3s, is also more likely to have greater amounts of environmental contaminants. Still, there are precautions you can take to reduce your risk of eating contaminated fish.

• Eat fish from a variety of sources.

• Opt for open-ocean fish and farmed fish over freshwater fish; they are less likely to harbor toxins.

• Eat smaller, younger fish. Older fish are more likely to have accumulated chemicals in their fatty tissues.

• Before you cast or drop your line, check the state's advisories for the waters you intend to fish to see if they advise limiting or avoiding consumption of fish from those waters. Try the state's department of public health, environment, or conservation; see government listings in your local phone directory.

• Don't make a habit of eating your catch if you fish in the same area over and over. Either vary the bodies of water from which you take fish, or eat your catch only occasionally.

• Avoid swordfish, shark, king mackerel, and tilefish, which are likely to be heavily contaminated with mercury.

Omega-3s have also shown promise in easing symptoms of rheumatoid arthritis because of their anti-inflammatory properties. Again, adding fish to the menu just two to three times a week has been suggested as a sound starting point.

You don't have to buy fresh to get the health benefits that omega-3 fatty acids offer. Canned fish, including tuna, sardines, and salmon, offer the same omega-3s as fresh varieties.

SELECTION AND STORAGE

Fish doesn't stay fresh long. If handled properly, fatty fish, such as bluefish, tuna, salmon, mackerel, or herring, lasts only about a week after leaving the water; lean fish, such as cod, haddock, or perch, lasts about ten days. To be sure the fish you buy is fresh, check for a "fishy" smell. If you detect one, don't buy it. Whether you buy whole fish, fish fillets, or steaks, the fish should be firm, not soft, to the touch. The scales should be shiny and clean, not slimy. Check the eyes; they should be clear, not cloudy, and should be bulging, not sunken. Fish fillets and steaks should be moist; steer clear if they look dried or curled around the edges.

It's best to cook fresh fish the same day you buy it. (Fish generally spoils faster than beef or chicken, and whole fish generally keeps better than steaks or fillets.) But it will keep in the refrigerator overnight if you place it in a plastic bag over a bowl of ice. If you need to keep it longer, freeze it. The quality of the fish is better retained if the fish is frozen quickly, so it's best to freeze fish whole only if it weighs two pounds or less. Larger fish should be cut into pieces, steaks, or fillets. Lean fish will keep in the freezer for up to six months; fatty fish, only about three months.

PREPARATION AND SERVING TIPS

Preparing fish without adding lots of fat is simple. The key to keeping fish moist and flavorful lies in taking advantage of fish's natural fat and juices. The number one rule: Preserve moistness. In practical terms, that means avoiding direct heat, especially when preparing lean fish. You'll get the best results with lean fish, such as flounder, monkfish, pike, and red snapper, if you use moist-heat methods, including poaching, steaming, or baking with vegetables or a sauce that holds moisture in. Dry-heat methods, such as baking, broiling, and grilling, work well for fattier fish.

Fish cooks fast. That means that it can overcook quickly. You can tell fish is done when it looks opaque and the flesh just begins to flake with the touch of a fork. The general rule of thumb for cooking fish is to cook ten minutes per inch of thickness, measured at the fish's thickest point.

Marinades do wonders for fish. But as with poultry, keep safety in mind. Never marinate at room temperature; only in the refrigerator. And never use the marinade as a sauce for prepared fish unless you boil the marinade first.

Legumes (Dried Beans and Peas)

Legumes are a staple food all over the world. Dried beans and peas are one of the best sources of soluble fiber. Plus, they're low in fat and high in good quality protein—a great health-saving combination. Beans can be gassy, of course, but there are ways around that. So don't let their "explosive" nature scare you away from some of the best nutrition around.

The soluble fiber in beans helps lower levels of damaging LDL cholesterol in the blood, thus lowering heart-disease risk. And by slowing down carbohydrate absorption, soluble bean fiber fends off unwanted peaks and valleys in blood glucose levels—especially valuable to people with diabetes. Beans also provide substantial insoluble fiber, which can keep constipation and other digestive woes away.

Legumes are also rich in folic acid, copper, iron, and magnesium—four nutrients many of us could use more of in our diets. In addition, dried beans and peas are generally good sources of iron, which is especially helpful for people who don't eat meat.

SELECTION AND STORAGE

Dried beans are available year-round, are inexpensive, and can be found in any well-stocked grocery. You may need to visit a health-food store for more exotic varieties, such as Oriental azuki (or adzuki) beans, flageolets, cranberry beans, or yellow split peas.

If stored properly, dried beans and peas will last for a year or more. Keep them in their unopened bag. After opening, store the beans in a dry, tightly closed glass jar in a cool, dark spot.

Note, too, that many varieties of beans are available already cooked and canned.

PREPARATION AND SERVING TIPS

When cooking with dried varieties of legumes, it's best to plan ahead. Before soaking or cooking, sort through the beans, discarding bad beans, pebbles, and debris. Then rinse the beans in cold water. It's best to soak your beans overnight, for six to eight hours; they'll cook faster and you'll get rid of gas-producing carbohydrates. But if you haven't planned far enough ahead, you can quick-soak for one hour. Quick-soak by putting the beans in water and boiling for one minute; then turn off the heat and let the beans stand in the same water for one hour. You may end up with a less-firm bean, however.

After soaking, discard any beans that float to the top, then throw out the soaking water and add fresh water to cook in. Add enough water to cover the beans plus two inches. Bring to a boil, then simmer, covered, until tender—about one to three hours, depending on the bean variety. They're done when you can easily stick them with a fork. Remember, cooked beans double or triple in volume.

Beans are notoriously bland-tasting, but that's what makes them versatile. They can take on the spices of any flavorful dish. Add them to soups, stews, salads, casseroles, and dips.

Nuts

This category is just a little nutty. It encompasses some foods that aren't true nuts but have been given honorary status due to their similar nutritional qualities. These include the peanut (really a legume), the Brazil nut, and the cashew (both technically seeds).

If you've relegated nuts to special occasions only, then it's time to reconsider. While they may be high in fat, nuts contain mostly mono- and polyunsaturated fats—fats with a heart-friendly reputation. In one study, people who ate nuts—almonds, cashews, pistachios, walnuts, or peanuts—five or more times a week were half as likely to have a heart attack or suffer from heart disease as people who rarely or never ate nuts. This protective effect may be attributable to the healthy fat profile of nuts, or it may be the result of the vitamin E and fiber found in nuts, both of which can help stave off heart disease; perhaps it's these several attributes combined and even other as yet unidentified ones that played a role. Other studies have demonstrated that adults with a high blood cholesterol level can lower both their total and LDL cholesterol levels by substituting nuts for other snack foods.

Besides being rich in protein, nuts offer a host of other nutrients, such as folate, phosphorus, magnesium, copper, zinc, and selenium. Another bonus—nuts are so dense with nutrients that they quell hunger pangs with fewer calories compared with other snack foods that often provide calories with minimal nutrition.

SELECTION AND STORAGE

Most fresh nuts are available only in the fall and winter. Shelled nuts can be purchased anytime. Look for a freshness date on the package or container. If you can, check to be sure there aren't a lot of shriveled or discolored nuts. Be wary if you buy your nuts in bulk; they should smell fresh, not rancid.

A caution: Aflatoxin, a known carcinogen produced by a mold that grows naturally on peanuts, can be a problem. Discard peanuts that are discolored, shriveled, or moldy or that taste bad. And stick to commercial brands of peanut butter. A survey found that best-selling brands contained only trace amounts of aflatoxin, but supermarket brands had five times that much, and fresh-ground peanut butters—like those sold in health-food stores—averaged more than ten times as much as the best-selling brands.

Because of their high fat content, you must protect nuts from rancidity. Nuts in their shells can be kept for a few months in a cool, dry location. But once they've been shelled or their containers opened, the best way to preserve them is to refrigerate or freeze them.

PREPARATION AND SERVING TIPS

To munch on as a snack, nuts are pretty much a self-serve affair. For nuts that are tough to crack, use a nutcracker or even pliers. A nutpick is useful for walnuts. Brazil nuts open easier if you chill them first. Almonds can be peeled by boiling them, then dunking them in cold water.

In cooking and baking, it's easy to get the nutritional benefits of nuts without overdosing on fat and calories, because a small amount of nuts adds a lot of flavor. Nuts sprinkled on your cereal can boost your morning fiber intake. Peanut butter makes a great snack on apple wedges or celery or simply spread on a piece of hearty whole-wheat toast. Walnuts go well tossed in Waldorf salad or with orange sections and spinach. Almonds dress up almost any vegetable when sprinkled on top. Nuts give grains extra pizzazz and crunch. Pignoli, or pine nuts, add a dash of Mediterranean flavor when included in pasta dishes; they're the nuts you'll find in your pesto dishes. Nuts stirred into yogurt make it a more satisfying light meal. And spice-cake and quick-bread mixes as well as pancake batters produce extra-special results when nuts are added in.

Seeds

Seeds are the "eggs" that contain the nutrients

needed to nourish the growth of a new plant. So their high nutrient content shouldn't come as a surprise. What's surprising is that we generally relegate these nutritional wonders to the occasional snack rather than making them staples of our diet.

With their gold mine of healthy minerals and their niacin and folic-acid contents, seeds are an excellent nutrition package. They are among the better plant sources of iron and zinc. In fact, one ounce of pumpkin seeds contains almost twice as much iron as three ounces of skinless chicken breast. And they provide more fiber per ounce than nuts. They are also good sources of protein. Sesame seeds are a surprising source of the bone-building mineral calcium, great news for folks who have trouble tolerating dairy products. And seeds are a rich source of vitamin E. The only drawback: Some seeds are quite high in fat. Sunflower and sesame seeds provide about 80 percent of their calories as fat, although the fat is mostly of the heart-smart unsaturated variety.

SELECTION AND STORAGE

Seeds are often sold in bulk, either with their hulls (shells) in place or with their kernels separated out. Make sure the seeds you buy are fresh. Because of their high fat content, seeds are vulnerable to rancidity. If they're exposed to heat, light, or humidity, they're likely to become rancid much faster. A quick sniff of the seed bin should tell you if the contents are fresh or not. Seeds that still have their hulls intact should keep for several months if you store them in a cool, dry location. Seed kernels (seeds that have had their shells removed) will keep for a slightly shorter period of time.

Pumpkin and squash seeds are similar in appearance—both have a relatively thin hull that is white to yellowish in color. (Hulled pumpkin seeds are a popular ingredient in Mexican cooking.) Pumpkin-seed kernels are medium-dark green in color. Sunflower seeds are easily recognized with their hard black-and-white-striped hull.

Preparation and Serving Tips

You can't go overboard with seeds because of their high fat content. But, in moderation, seeds can be mixed with cereals or trail mix or eaten by themselves. A sprinkling of seed kernels over fruits, vegetables, pastas, or salads adds a touch of crunchy texture and flavor. Sesame seeds are especially attractive as toppers for breads, rolls, salads, and stir-fries.

MILK, YOGURT, AND CHEESE

Foods in this group supply approximately 75 percent of the calcium we consume. In addition, they provide protein, phosphorus, potassium, and vitamins A, D, B_{12}, and riboflavin. Although milk, yogurt, and cheese offer significant amounts of calcium and other key nutrients, most people eat only half the recommended daily servings from this group. That means many people—adults and children—may not be getting enough calcium and other nutrients essential to staying healthy. Certainly, foods from other groups contain calcium, but foods outside this group generally contain less, and the body may not absorb it as well.

Calcium for Health

It is well known that calcium plays some pivotal roles in maintaining good health—from keeping bones healthy and strong and helping prevent high blood pressure to more recent findings that the calcium in dairy products may make it easier to lose weight. Calcium also helps your blood to clot and keeps your muscles and nerves working properly. If your body doesn't get enough calcium from food, it steals calcium from your bones to help keep a steady amount in your blood. Fortunately, it can be fairly easy to meet your daily calcium needs if you regularly enjoy milk, yogurt, and cheese.

The Sunshine Vitamin

Vitamin D is an essential nutrient for building and maintaining strong bones and teeth. It is a unique vitamin—your body can make its own vitamin D when sunlight makes contact with your skin. To get enough, it only takes a few minutes of sun exposure, three times a week, on your hands, arms, or face (without sunscreen). However, if you live in Northern climates or don't get outdoors much, especially in the winter, you should not rely on sunshine. Also, as you age, your body may not be as efficient at making vitamin D, so food sources become even more important.

Your most reliable source of vitamin D is milk. Although milk is fortified with the vitamin, dairy products made from milk such as cheese, yogurt, and ice cream are generally not fortified with vitamin D. Only a few foods, including fatty fish and fish oils, naturally contain significant amounts of vitamin D. Other foods that contain smaller amounts of vitamin D include eggs, fortified breakfast cereals, and margarine.

Serving Up Dairy

To meet your calcium requirements, most people should have about three cups of dairy foods each day. Teens have the highest calcium requirements and should get about four cups daily. Each of the following equals one cup of dairy:

- 1 cup milk

- 1 cup yogurt

CALCIUM AT EVERY AGE AND STAGE

Age (years)	Daily Calcium Needs (milligrams)
1–3	500
4–8	800
9–18	1,300
19–50	1,000
51 and older	1,200
Pregnant/breast-feeding woman	1,000
Pregnant/breast-feeding teen (less than 18 years of age)	1,300

- 1½ ounces natural cheese (cheddar, Swiss, Monterey Jack, etc.)
- 2 ounces processed cheese (American)
- ½ cup evaporated milk
- 1 cup pudding
- ½ cup ricotta cheese
- 1 cup frozen yogurt
- 2 cups cottage cheese
- 1½ cups ice cream

Note: For some of these, such as frozen yogurt, cottage cheese, and ice cream, a typical or reasonable portion is smaller than the amount that equals a one-cup serving—for example, you're more likely to have only one cup of cottage cheese in a sitting—so count your actual portion for what it is, such as half a serving in the cottage cheese example. *Also note:* Other dairy-based foods, such as butter, cream cheese, and sour cream, are *not* considered dairy servings. These foods are made from the cream portion of milk and contain mostly fat and little, if any, calcium.

Versatile Milk

There are many varieties of milk—with different flavors and nutrition profiles. The easiest way to enjoy milk is ice-cold with a meal or snack. Most types of milk have about the same amount of calcium, protein, and most other nutrients per cup. The main differences are in calories and fat.

Obviously, you're better off nutritionally if you choose fat-free, or at least 1 percent, milk to

1 CUP	CALCIUM (MG)	CALORIES	FAT (G)
Fat-free (skim) milk	300	80	0
Low-fat (½%) milk	300	90	1
Low-fat (1%) milk	300	100	2.5
Low-fat (1%) chocolate milk	290	160	2.5
Low-fat (1%) buttermilk	280	100	2.5
Reduced-fat (2%) milk	300	120	5
Whole (3.25% fat) milk	300	150	8

keep fat and excess calories to a minimum. However, if you have children under the age of two, give them whole milk. Young, rapidly growing children need the calories and fat that whole milk provides.

You might also want to give buttermilk a try. With its distinctively tart, sour taste, it's not for everyone, but many people prefer its flavor. Buttermilk is not as fattening as it sounds. Though originally a by-product of butter, today buttermilk is made by adding bacteria cultures to fat-free or low-fat milk. Read the carton to be sure you're getting the low- or nonfat variety. Buttermilk tends to be saltier than regular milk, however (a concern if you have or are at risk for high blood pressure), and it may not be fortified with vitamins A and D.

BEYOND STRAIGHT UP

There are other ways to include milk beyond drinking it plain:

• Many recipes call for milk, and in others, you can easily substitute milk for water. For example, use milk to make hot cereals; pancakes and waffles; soups; packaged potato, pasta, and rice mixes; baked goods; desserts; and drink mixes.

• Cereal and a cup of milk makes a good anytime snack—and it meets about a third of your daily requirement for calcium.

• Try blending milk with yogurt, fruit, and ice cubes for a refreshing fruit smoothie. Add a flavor twist by using chocolate-, banana-, vanilla-, or strawberry-flavored milk.

• Have some coffee with your milk. Try a café latte

or cappuccino to get a healthy amount of milk with your coffee.

• If you're a soda drinker, consider choosing fat-free milk instead of regular soda once in a while to save about 90 calories and get milk's nine essential nutrients.

MILK STORAGE

All milk should have a "sell by" date stamped on the carton. This date is the last day the milk should be sold if it is to remain fresh for home storage. It does not mean that you need to use it by that date. Generally, if milk is stored in a closed container at refrigerator temperatures, it will remain fresh for up to a week after the "sell by" date. Pasteurization—the process of rapidly heating raw milk, holding it for a short specified period of time, then rapidly cooling it—removes most of the bacteria from milk. However, some of the remaining harmless bacteria can grow and multiply, although very slowly, at refrigerator temperatures, eventually causing the milk to spoil.

Store milk on a refrigerator shelf rather than in the door, which is not cold enough. To safeguard quality and freshness, store milk in the original container. Keep milk containers closed and away from strong-smelling foods. To avoid cross-contaminating milk, do not return unused milk from a serving pitcher to the original container. If milk has been left at room temperature for longer than two hours, throw it out.

Milk in plastic jugs is more susceptible to loss of riboflavin and vitamin A than milk in paperboard cartons. That's because light, even the fluorescent light in supermarkets, destroys these two light-sensitive nutrients.

Today, you may find milk not only in the refrigerated section but also out on the shelf with packaged goods. This is called UHT (ultra-high-temperature) milk, referring to the processing technique. Though it must be refrigerated once you open it, unopened UHT milk will keep at room temperature for up to six months. UHT milk is just as nutritious as the milk you buy in the refrigerated section.

Drinking raw milk, or products that are made with raw milk such as some cheeses, can be risky. Raw milk has not been pasteurized and often carries bacteria that can make you sick. It's especially dangerous to give raw milk to children, the elderly, or people with impaired immune systems.

Cheese, Please

Cheese can be made from whole, low-fat, or skim milk or combinations of these. Regardless of the type of milk used to create it, cheese is a concentrated source of the nutrients naturally found in milk, including calcium. Indeed, many cheeses provide 200 to 300 milligrams of calcium per ounce.

"Low-fat cheese" used to be an oxymoron. No more. Today, there are dozens of reduced-fat, low-fat, and fat-free versions of American, cheddar, mozzarella, Swiss, and other cheeses that you may find worth biting into. Fat in this new generation of cheeses has been cut anywhere from 25 to 100 percent. The average fat reduction is about 30 percent. Most of these contain added gums and stabilizers that help simulate the creamy texture and rich taste of full-fat cheeses.

The taste and texture of lower-fat cheeses vary considerably. Some people find them fine substitutes for the full-fat varieties, while other folks don't, preferring to forgo cheese rather than settle for a low-fat substitute. Cheese connoisseurs will probably never be true fans of reduced-fat cheeses, but if you're trying to cut back on saturated fat and cholesterol, they do offer alternatives.

The one nutritional drawback of reduced-fat cheeses is that they are usually higher in sodium than full-fat natural cheeses. An ounce of regular Swiss cheese, for example, contains only about 74 milligrams of sodium. A reduced-fat Swiss may contain 300 to 400 milligrams or more per ounce.

Are reduced-fat cheeses the answer for a diet hopelessly high in fat? Hardly. Unless you're a big cheese eater, chances are other elements of your diet—such as fatty meats, whole milk, buttery muffins and croissants, chips, and ice cream—are more in need of a good fat-trimming. But substituting reduced-fat for full-fat cheese can't hurt. When it comes to the war on fat, every gram counts.

Another option for cheese lovers is to use strong-flavored cheeses, such as Parmesan, blue, or gorgonzola. With these, a little can go a long way in terms of adding flavor.

CHEESE SELECTION AND STORAGE

Many cheeses have considerably more fat per serving than a cup of milk. When shopping for lower-fat cheeses, here's what the label will tell you:

• Low-fat cheese: three grams or less of fat per one-ounce serving

• Reduced-fat cheese: 25 percent less fat than the same full-fat cheese

• Fat-free cheese: less than 0.5 gram of fat per one-ounce serving

For reduced-fat cheeses, opt for varieties that provide no more than five grams of fat per ounce. Regular cheeses provide eight to nine grams per ounce. Brands vary a lot in taste and texture. Shop around until you find one you like. You're better off choosing a reduced-fat cheese based on taste and then trying it in recipes. Remember, the less fat a cheese contains, the harder it is to use in cooking.

Because of their high moisture content, lower-fat cheeses turn moldy more quickly than their full-fat counterparts. Keep them well wrapped in the refrigerator, and use them as soon as possible.

COOKING WITH CHEESE

In general, the further you get from traditional cheese in terms of fat content, the more careful you have to be about applying heat. It's the high fat content of regular cheese, generally about 70 percent of its calories, that gives full-fat cheese its smooth, creamy texture and allows it to melt easily. When you reduce the fat content, the cheese becomes less pliable and more difficult to melt. The lower the fat content, the tougher the melting problem becomes. Trying to make a cheese sauce with a reduced-fat cheese can truly be an exercise in futility because the product is prone to breaking down into a clumpy, stringy mess.

Nonfat cheeses are best served "as is" in unheated sandwiches or in salads. They generally have milder flavors than regular cheeses and sometimes have what cheese purists sometimes describe as slightly "off" flavors.

To lighten the calorie and fat load of recipes without dramatically altering the flavor or texture, try replacing one-half to two-thirds of a full-fat cheese with a reduced-fat variety. Grated cheese blends best. Or combine a small amount of full-fat, full-bodied cheese like extra sharp cheddar or Parmesan with a reduced-fat cheese. A little full-fat cheese can go a long way toward improving the flavor of the dish. Most reduced-fat cheeses melt smoothly when they are layered in a casserole; the layers serve as insulation and help prevent the cheese from separating or becoming stringy.

The lower the amount of fat in a cheese, the longer it takes to melt and the more likely it is to produce a "skin" and scorch when baked. To counter this problem, top casseroles and baked pasta dishes with reduced-fat cheese only near the end of the baking time, and heat until just melted. Serve immediately.

Meltability on top of dishes like casseroles or pizzas varies among varieties of reduced-fat cheeses just as it does among traditional cheeses. You may find, for example, that a fat-reduced mozzarella melts much more smoothly than a fat-reduced cheddar. Meltability, texture, and taste may also vary among brands within a variety. Therefore, you'll probably need to do some shopping around and some experimenting to determine which varieties and which brands suit your needs and tastes in various situations; you'll probably prefer some kinds for snacking and other kinds for cooking or as toppings.

Say "Yes" to Yogurt

Yogurt was a long-established staple in Eastern Europe and the Middle East before it reached our shores. And there was a time when yogurt eaters in this country were considered "health nuts." Our attitudes have changed considerably. Today, yogurt is commonly consumed by men, women, and children of all ages. Walk into any supermarket today, and you'll see the varieties and flavors of this nutritious food take up considerable space in the dairy section.

FRIENDLY BACTERIA

Yogurt may not be the miracle food some have

claimed, but it certainly has a lot to offer in the health department. Besides being an excellent source of bone-building calcium, it is believed that the bacterial cultures *Lactobacillus bulgaricus* (*L. bulgaricus*) and *Streptococcus thermophilus* (*S. thermophilus*), that are used to make yogurt, carry their own health benefits.

For example, research has suggested that eating yogurt regularly helps boost the body's immune-system function, warding off colds and possibly even helping to fend off cancer. It is also thought the friendly bacteria found in many types of yogurt can help prevent and even remedy diarrhea.

For people who suffer from lactose intolerance, yogurt is often well tolerated because live yogurt cultures produce lactase, making the lactose sugar in the yogurt easier to digest (see Lactose Intolerance for advice on coping with this condition). Be sure to check the label on the yogurt carton for the National Yogurt Association's Live and Active Cultures (LAC) seal. This seal identifies products that contain a significant amount of live and active cultures. But don't look to frozen yogurt as an option; most frozen yogurt contains little of the healthful bacteria.

YOGURT SELECTION AND STORAGE

There is a dizzying array of brands and flavors and varieties of yogurts in most supermarkets. But there are some basic traits to look for when deciding which to put in your grocery cart. Choose a yogurt that is either low fat or fat free. It should contain no more than three grams of fat per eight-ounce carton. Some yogurts are also sugar free (these are often signaled by the term "light," but check the label carefully to be sure, since this term might also refer to fat content) and contain an alternative sweetener instead of added sugar. Consider choosing plain, vanilla, lemon, or any one of the yogurts without a jamlike fruit mixture added. The mixture adds mainly calories and little if anything in the way of vitamins, minerals, or fiber. Your best health bet is to add your own fresh fruit to plain fat-free yogurt.

Yogurt must always be refrigerated. Each carton should have a "sell by" date stamped on it. It should be eaten within the week following the "sell by" date to take full advantage of the live and active cultures in the yogurt. As yogurt is stored, the amount of live and active cultures begins to decline.

PREPARATION AND SERVING TIPS

Yogurt can be enjoyed as a low-fat dessert, snack, or meal accompaniment; just add sliced berries, nuts, wheat germ, bananas, peaches, fruit cocktail, mandarin-orange slices, pineapple chunks, low-fat granola, or bran cereal. Yogurt also works well as a low-fat substitute in a lot of recipes that call for high-fat ingredients such as sour cream or cream. Yogurt is especially well-suited as a base for vegetable and/or chip dips and salad dressings.

PART III

✳ ✳ ✳

THE POWER OF HERBAL MEDICATION

HERBAL MEDICINE

✳ ✳ ✳

Modern medicine owes an enormous debt of gratitude to herbal medicine, the ultimate original source of many of today's drugs. There are thousands of medicinal herbs, and they contain an array of health-improving compounds that work together in ways we have only just begun to comprehend. Herbs have an amazing range of beneficial effects, and they rarely cause side effects. And herbs are usually quite inexpensive, a definite plus as the cost of prescription drugs continues to sky-rocket.

Some of the herbs discussed here are commonplace; you use them in cooking or in tea. Others may sound more exotic. But all of them will help improve the conditions reviewed in Part I, and most have other health benefits, too. The herbs selected have a very long history of use, and some have been the subject of rigorous research. We also focus here on herbs that can be grown in America, as it is environmentally sustainable to use what is nearby rather than having to ship it in from far away.

Ginger

Ginger is one of the ancient, revered medicines of India and Asia. The list of conditions for which it is used is so long, that it might prompt skepticism. How can one herb affect so many seemingly different diseases?

HEALING PROPERTIES

Ginger's ability to benefit a variety of diseases and conditions is due in part to its impact on excessive inflammation, which is a significant underlying cause of many illnesses. Inflammation is the body's natural healing response to illness or injury, and its pain, redness, heat, and swelling are attempts to keep you from moving a damaged area while it is being repaired. Inflammation subsides as the body heals. However, in some conditions, including arthritis, diverticulosis, gallbladder inflammation, and heart disease, the inflammation does not go away. It becomes chronic and leads to many other problems.

Ginger is particularly useful in treating chronic inflammation because it partially inhibits two important enzymes that play a role in inflammation gone awry—cyclooxygenase (COX) and 5-lipoxygenase (LOX). While anti-inflammatory drugs block COX more strongly, they don't affect LOX at all and therefore only address part of the problem. Even worse, anti-inflammatory drugs can cause side effects, such as ulcers, because they also block the beneficial effects that COX has on the digestive tract, including protecting the stomach. Ginger does not cause stomach irritation; instead it helps protect and heal the gut. Ginger also treats a broader range of the inflammatory problem because it affects both the COX and the LOX enzymes. And because it doesn't shut down the inflammatory process entirely, ginger may actually allow it to work properly and then turn itself off, the way it does with an injury.

Besides reducing inflammation, ginger has many other benefits. It helps relieve nausea, destroys a host of viruses, and in some laboratory studies has shown promise as an anticancer agent.

PREPARATION AND DOSAGE

The part of ginger we use is not a root, as one might guess from the way it looks. It's actually the rhizome, or underground stem. The spicy, aromatic compounds in the rhizome that impart the medicinal activity to ginger are relatively susceptible to heat and oxygen, so tread gingerly when making medicine from this herb.

To make a tea, cut a two-inch cube of rhizome into slices and simmer them in one cup of water on low heat for 10 minutes. Cover the pot while cooking to retain as many volatile constituents as possible. Remove the slices, and sip the remaining liquid before a meal. Eat the slices after drinking the tea. Drink three cups of tea per day, one before each meal.

Ginger capsules or powder are also widely available. Take at least 2,000 mg three times or more per day with or without food. Just be sure to use powder that has not been sitting around too long, as it can lose its potency.

People often make the mistake of taking too little ginger and thus don't gain the full benefits.

PRECAUTIONS

Ginger is extremely safe. Some people have trouble tolerating its spiciness, but most tend to adapt if they keep taking it. Some concern has been raised because ginger may block platelets from sticking together and cause bleeding, but there have been no cases reported of bleeding in people taking ginger. However, do not take ginger with blood thinners without first consulting your health care professional. Ginger is safe to use for short-term use (a few days) in pregnancy.

STORAGE

Store fresh ginger rhizomes in a cool, dark, dry place. Do not keep them in the refrigerator, even after cutting them, or they will shrivel up. Use within 2 to 3 weeks for optimal effects. Capsules or powder should be kept away from heat and light.

Garlic

Garlic and ginger are classified as both foods and medicinal herbs. Both can and should be eaten as food, but they can also be taken in supplement form to augment a healthy diet when more serious health problems arise.

HEALING PROPERTIES

Garlic has many healing properties, but the most research has been done on its potential to help reduce heart disease. Garlic has

THE POTENTIAL OF ALLICIN

Good quality garlic supplements list the "allicin potential" they contain and not a certain amount of allicin. This means that when the supplement gets to the stomach, it releases 6,000 mcg of allicin, the pungent chemical that accounts for garlic's sharp flavor. The supplements do not contain actual allicin, because this compound is extremely unstable and quickly breaks down. Instead, good garlic supplements contain alliin, the stable precursor to allicin. It is released only upon digestion, so your body can make the best use of it.

been intensively studied, and numerous large studies have shown that taking supplements that mimic fresh garlic can significantly lower LDL cholesterol levels without hurting beneficial HDL cholesterol levels. Garlic appears to act by blocking the liver from making too much LDL cholesterol (see Heart Disease and Stroke, page 72, for more information). There is also some evidence that garlic supplements can mildly lower blood pressure by dilating or expanding blood vessels. And garlic helps prevent blood clots—and therefore reduces the risk of heart attack and stroke—by decreasing the stickiness of platelets, which are tiny disk-shaped bodies in the blood that are necessary for blood clotting. When platelets are too sticky, they form clumps that can adhere to artery walls and contribute to clogged arteries.

Garlic has also been shown to reduce pain and other symptoms in people with rheumatoid arthritis. And it reduces the size of some cancerous tumors and helps prevent some cancers, particularly those in the intestines. However, the research on this is not nearly as far advanced as that for garlic and heart disease, so do not use garlic supplements without consulting with a natural health care professional.

One of the oldest uses of garlic, however, is as an antibiotic. Garlic kills a range of microbes, including viruses, bacteria, fungi, and parasites, and so can be effective against such conditions as athlete's foot, thrush (a fungal infection of the mouth), viral diarrhea, and the ulcer-causing bacteria *Helicobacter pylori*. Only fresh garlic or supplements that mimic it have these effects.

PREPARATION AND DOSAGE

For best results, fresh garlic or preparations that mimic it need to be used. Dried or cooked garlic, as well as garlic oil, lose a significant amount of potency during processing (though they aren't worthless and are still beneficial to eat as food). Preparations used for medicinal purposes should state that they have allicin potential (see The Potential of Allicin, page 189) of at least 6,000 mcg on the label. Alternately, eat one chopped clove of fresh garlic per day. (The fresh garlic that has been peeled and sometimes minced and sold in jars in the grocery store is not potent enough.)

PRECAUTIONS

Garlic is safe, but it makes the breath and sweat smell

rather unpleasant. If it doesn't make you odiferous, then it wasn't very useful, since the smell indicates the presence of the healing properties. To help reduce the odor, take a source of chlorophyll, such as a fresh leafy green vegetable or parsley, with garlic. Or take most of your garlic at night, then shower in the morning.

A more serious but rare side effect is spontaneous bleeding, either from taking too much garlic or taking it with blood thinner medications. Do not exceed the dose indicated above and do not take it with these drugs without consulting a natural health care professional. Garlic is safe for short-term use in pregnancy.

STORAGE
Store garlic in a cool, dark, dry place with good air

circulation. Check on it occasionally, and remove any cloves that have gone bad, being careful not to nick the remaining cloves.

Oregon Grape
Oregon grape and its cousin goldenseal act very similarly. But since Oregon grape is easy to grow and is not threatened with extinction, more and more herbal practitioners are switching from goldenseal to Oregon grape to treat a range of conditions.

HEALING PROPERTIES
Oregon grape root has a distinctly bitter taste due to the presence of alkaloids, including berberine, the most notable. Though initially disagreeable to people not familiar with bitter herbs, these substances have a beneficial effect on the digestive

tract. They stimulate the flow of bile, which loosens the stools and helps prevent and sometimes relieves constipation, diverticulosis, gallbladder disease, and hemorrhoids. They may also help people with constipation-predominant irritable bowel syndrome (IBS).

Oregon grape also has antibiotic and anticancer properties that are receiving more and more attention by researchers and clinicians. Berberine and other alkaloids have been shown to kill a wide range of microbes and have been effective in human studies for speeding recovery from giardia, candida, viral diarrhea, and cholera. Studies in China show that an alkaloid it contains, called berbamine, helps protect the bone marrow and promotes its recovery from chemother-

apy and radiation therapy for cancer. Combined with its bitter digestive-strengthening properties, Oregon grape has an interesting and distinctive combination of properties.

PREPARATION AND DOSAGE

Oregon grape root is taken either as a tea or tincture. To make tea, simmer 1 to 2 teaspoons dried, coarsely chopped root in 1 cup water for 10 to 15 minutes. Strain out the leftover root (or eat it, if you prefer), and sip the remaining liquid just before eating each substantial meal.

A tincture is an alcohol extract of the root. Mix ½ to 1 teaspoon in 2 to 4 ounces of water and sip before each meal. The amount of alcohol in tinctures at this dose is very low and presents no significant problem.

PRECAUTIONS

The bitterness of Oregon grape root makes some people nauseous when they first start taking it, though this usually passes after the first few doses. Do not take Oregon grape root if you have chronic diarrhea, a duodenal ulcer, or excessive stomach acid, as it could make these conditions worse. Do not take Oregon grape root in pregnancy without first consulting with a natural health care professional.

STORAGE

Keep dried Oregon grape root away from light and heat. Do not keep longer than one year. Tincture will keep indefinitely if stored away from light and heat.

Nettle

Nettle delivers a painful sting, so hikers tend to steer clear of it. But the leaves of this prickly herb pack a range of health-benefiting properties.

HEALING PROPERTIES

Nettle is particularly effective as a diuretic, so it helps prevent most types of kidney stones as well as urinary tract infections. By keeping water flowing through the kidneys and bladder, nettle helps keep crystals from forming into stones and washes bacteria away.

Nettle is distinctly different from diuretic drugs. These drugs are often used to reduce high blood pressure and edema (swelling from excessive fluid), but studies have not shown nettle to help either of these conditions. It's unclear why this is the case. It may be that the herb works differently than diuretic drugs, or it may simply be that the correct research has not yet been done.

Nettle leaves can also help reduce the pain of arthritis. In one preliminary study, nettle leaf juice was as effective at reducing the pain of various types of arthritis as anti-inflammatory drugs. In another study, nettle leaf juice enhanced the effects of the anti-inflammatory drug diclofenac in people with osteoarthritis.

In addition to drinking nettle leaf tea or juice, an old tradition for relieving the pain of arthritis is to apply fresh leaves over aching joints. Though this initially causes increased pain from the stings, it ultimately relieves inflammation and pain. This effect may be the result of something known as the "gate phenomenon."

When the skin over a painful joint is stung, the spinal cord reduces pain signals coming from the joint underneath. Two studies have now shown that the application of topical nettle stings is in fact helpful for relieving arthritis pain for those who can tolerate the initial discomfort. Taking nettle by mouth in any of its forms, including capsules or tinctures, is also helpful for arthritis.

PREPARATION AND DOSAGE

Drinking nettle leaf tea or juice is the best way to use nettles for diuretic purposes. To make tea, combine 2 to 3 teaspoons dried leaf (which doesn't sting) with 1 cup hot water, and allow to steep 10 to 15 minutes. Drink 1 cup tea three times per day. If you prefer to drink juice, take 1 to 2 ounces fresh nettle leaf juice three times per day. Another option is to take capsules providing 2 to 3 grams of the herb or 5 mL tincture or glycerite three times per day. To apply topically, put 2 to 3 fresh leaves on small joints such as the fingers and elbows or 4 to 6 fresh leaves on larger joints such as knees and ankles two to three times per day. Remove them a minute or two after application, once multiple stings have occurred. Fresh leaves can be reused, as long as they keep stinging and don't rot.

PRECAUTIONS

Nettle is very safe. It is even safe for children and pregnant women, though topical application is not. People with allergies or severe reactions to the stings should not use the herb.

Do not use nettle to treat an acute kidney stone attack or a bladder infection without close monitoring by a health care professional. Both conditions can be serious and nettle alone cannot resolve these problems.

STORAGE

Dried nettle leaf should be stored in an airtight container, away from light and heat. It will last as long as a year if protected. Fresh leaves to use for topical stings are difficult to come by. You must either grow them in the garden or have a nearby source to harvest them from the wild. Keep fresh nettles in a plastic bag in the refrigerator.

American Ginseng

American ginseng root is one of the most prized herbs in the world.

In fact, it is most revered in China, even though an almost identical herb, called Asian ginseng, is native there. By the same token, in the United States, Asian ginseng is considered by some to be superior, although there is no evidence of that. Asian ginseng simply sounds more exotic.

HEALING PROPERTIES

Research on American ginseng root in the past 20 years has increasingly shown that it can help lower blood sugar in people with diabetes mellitus. The effect seems most prominent when American ginseng is taken 30 to 60 minutes before eating. This suggests American ginseng may work in part by slowing the absorption of sugars from the diet. Other research hints that American ginseng may work at least in part by making the cells more receptive to insulin in people who are insulin resistant.

Regardless of how American ginseng works, it must be used in conjunction with dietary and lifestyle changes (see Diabetes, page 53). American ginseng works well with these therapies but is not effective by itself. It may help avoid the need for oral diabetes drugs in people with type II diabetes but can never substitute for insulin in people with type I diabetes. However, there have been no long-term studies on this.

American ginseng also helps the body cope with stress and strengthens the immune system. Compounds known as saponins that are found in ginseng reduce the damage the body's stress hormones cause. Saponins may also help muscle cells produce and use energy more efficiently, which helps the body cope with stress. These compensatory mechanisms reduce the negative impact of stress on immunity.

Cancer cells tend to secrete compounds that inhibit the immune system, and there is some evidence that ginseng can reduce the immune-suppressing and immune-damaging effects of cancer and of treatments for cancer, such as surgery, chemotherapy, and radiation. This seems to improve quality of life, though its effect on longevity is not yet known. Ginseng also directly augments the effects of T helper cells, the leaders of the immune system, which are also quite helpful to cancer patients.

PREPARATION AND DOSAGE

Do not use wild American ginseng, as the plant is too rare. Instead, use what is known as wild-simulated or woods-cultivated American ginseng. In this growing method, American ginseng is planted in something approximating its normal forest habitat so that it ends up with properties very close to wild plants. Take capsules providing 2 to 3 grams of herb or 1 teaspoon of tincture 30 minutes before each meal.

PRECAUTIONS

American ginseng cannot take the place of insulin. In fact, it may cause insulin to lower blood sugar too much, so do not take American ginseng with insulin on your own. Consult a natural health care professional who can help you find a safe dose. The same is true for combining American ginseng with oral hypoglycemic medications, because it may cause them to lower blood sugar too much. American ginseng may also inhibit the ability of blood-clotting platelets to stick together. As a result, taking American ginseng with blood-thinning drugs may increase the risk of bleeding. Do not take blood thinners with American ginseng without consulting a health care professional.

STORAGE

Whole American ginseng root, protected from light, heat, and air, can remain potent for a very long time. Powdered root breaks down much more quickly and thus capsules should be taken very quickly. Tincture will keep indefinitely.

Peppermint

Peppermint is familiar because it is widely used as a flavoring in foods, beverages, and over-the-counter products.

HEALING PROPERTIES

Most people have heard about the benefits of peppermint leaf tea for relief of an upset stomach. Peppermint's reputation is due in large part to its volatile oil compounds that relax the smooth muscles that line the digestive tract. When these muscle cells become overactive, they contribute to indigestion, dyspepsia, gallbladder disease, and irritable bowel syndrome (IBS). Several clinical trials have also shown that peppermint essential oil, a superconcentrated form of the herb, can relieve irritable bowel syndrome (IBS) symptoms. If IBS symptoms persist despite peppermint use, seek a health care professional's help to be sure you don't have an ulcer or a more serious health problem.

Another series of research studies showed that menthol and closely related compounds from mint oils can actually dissolve gallstones; however, this may take many months to achieve. It is imperative to maintain a low-fat diet, lose weight, exercise regularly, and undertake the other measures discussed in the gallbladder disease profile at the same time to help the peppermint oil work best.

PREPARATION AND DOSAGE

Peppermint leaf tea is an excellent and safe way to use peppermint for occasional indigestion, mild IBS, or early stages of gallbladder disease. Steep 1 to 2 teaspoons of the herb or two tea bags in 1 cup hot water, covered, for 10 to 15 minutes. You should see a layer of oil on the top of the water when the tea is done. If you don't cover the tea while steeping, the oil—and the medicinal benefits—will escape into the air. Drink 1 cup tea (with the oil) a few minutes before each meal.

As an alternative, you can take 1 to 3 drops of peppermint essential oil three times per day. The oil can be purchased in a bottle or in capsules. Place the drops directly under the tongue. Another effective alternative is enteric-coated peppermint oil supplements. These deliver more of the essential oil to the intestines, where it is needed, and may help you avoid heartburn. Take 1 to 2 capsules (each of which should provide 0.2 mL menthol) three times per day.

PRECAUTIONS

In some people, peppermint can relax the muscles that help keep stomach acid from backing up into the esophagus, leading to heartburn. This effect may be worse in people who already have heartburn. Avoid taking peppermint at bedtime, as lying down increases the chance of acid reflux.

Peppermint oil is extremely concentrated and should be kept out of the reach of children. Overdose can cause severe nerve problems including seizures, especially in children. It is also flammable. Peppermint oil should not be taken in pregnancy. Peppermint tea is generally safe for pregnant women or children, but discontinue use if it causes heartburn.

STORAGE

Store dried peppermint leaf in an airtight container in a dark, dry, cool place to prolong its potency. Do the same for peppermint oil to prevent it from becoming oxidized and losing its effects.

Turkey Tail Mushroom (Coriolus, yun zhi)

Turkey tail mushroom, like other medicinal mushrooms, has long been esteemed in traditional Chinese medicine.

HEALING PROPERTIES

Its main effects are to strengthen the immune system, particularly by enhancing the workings of one of the most critical cells, known as T helper cells. T helper cells tell all the other cells in the immune system what to do and to what degree, and when to stop.

In cancer, the runaway cells often secrete compounds known as cytokines that give false signals to immune cells to stop working. This further enhances the ability of the cancer to survive. An unfortunate side effect of chemotherapy and radiation therapy is that they further damage the immune system, in part by inadvertently killing T helper cells.

Turkey tail mushroom has been the subject of a large number of controlled clinical trials in Asia showing that it can help rebuild the immune system in people with a wide range of cancers. The benefit is quite powerful, for it has been demonstrated again and again that turkey tail, taken together with mainstream cancer therapies, significantly lengthens lifespan by as much as double. Turkey tail is not a magic cure for cancer, but it can definitely extend life.

Turkey tail may also improve quality of life by reducing susceptibility to infections and other negative effects of having a suppressed immune system. More research is needed to quantify these effects, but they should not be overlooked, as living well is just as important as living.

Because of its positive effects on the immune system, it's possible that turkey tail mushroom could prevent cancer or help other conditions in which immune suppression is a major problem, such as human immunodeficiency virus (HIV) infection. Research has yet to be done to investigate turkey tail's potential promise.

PREPARATION AND DOSAGE

The usual dose is 2 to 3 grams of dried, powdered turkey tail mushrooms three times per day, either mixed into food or put into capsules. Specialized extracts known as PSK or PSP (which focus on single polysaccharides in the mushroom, to the exclusion of all other potentially beneficial compounds) were the actual form of this mushroom studied and are given in the same amounts as powdered turkey tail. However, these extracts are quite a bit more expensive than the whole powdered herb. Crude turkey tail mushroom has been used successfully in traditional medicine for thousands of years, so it is unlikely these special extracts must used for it to be effective.

PRECAUTIONS

No side effects from taking turkey tail have ever been reported in its many thousands of years of historical use or in modern research. Turkey tail should not be taken with immunosuppressive drugs, such as those prescribed to people with organ transplants, without first consulting a health care professional.

STORAGE

Turkey tail mushroom generally stays potent for many years, regardless of is form. The constituents don't break down easily. Keeping it away from heat and light will help extend its useful shelf life.

BUYING HERBAL PRODUCTS: WHAT YOU NEED TO KNOW

✕ ✕ ✕

Americans are accustomed to turning to pills for their medicine, so it may seem natural to take herbs in supplement form. But this is often not the optimal way to take herbs. Grinding an herb into powder often damages delicate medicinal constituents, shortening shelf life and reducing potency. Fresh herbs, recently dried herbs, and whole herbs chopped just before being eaten or made into tea are often quite a bit stronger and therefore more effective.

SAFETY AND QUALITY ISSUES

When you cannot obtain the fresh herb, your only option is to use an herbal supplement. Herbal products are widely available, yet unfortunately there are many companies that sell products of substandard quality and purity. Herbal products are considered dietary supplements by the Food and Drug Administration (FDA), and they are not subject to the same standards as prescription and nonprescription drugs. Manufacturers don't have to prove the safety and efficacy of herbal products before they put them on the market. They are only required to provide accurate information on the product's label about the contents, the quantity, the manufacturer, and the directions for use. In addition, the FDA requires a Supplement Facts panel that lists serving size, dietary and nondietary ingredients, and amount per serving size as well as the scientific name of the plant. However, there is insufficient enforcement to be sure that the herbs you buy (especially on the Internet) will do what you want—and that they won't do anything else.

Who Can You Trust?
Therefore, the safest way to obtain herbal products is to contact a knowledgeable natural health care practitioner who uses herbs clinically and can recommend legitimate herbal companies. For supplements of Western herbs, consult either a licensed naturopathic physician who is a member of the American Association of Naturopathic Physicians (AANP) or an herbalist who is a member of the American Herbalists Guild (AHG). These two organizations admit only highly qualified practitioners who have studied and learned to use Western herbal medicines safely and effectively. They are best able to steer you to safe products or companies.

An alternative is to shop at small, local herb stores. Large chains and health food stores that do not specialize in herbs or that are run by conglomerates are less likely to have consistently excellent quality. Small shops are mostly run by herbalists who love herbal medicine and pride themselves on the quality of their herbs. Most of them have spent many years studying and improving their skills. And while they, too, have a profit motive, it is much less likely to lead to them cut corners or sell inferior products.

Finally, herb companies that belong to the American Herbal Products Association (AHPA) are always the most reputable. This industry group requires its members to uphold higher standards than those mandated by U.S. laws.

ARE STANDARDIZED PRODUCTS BEST?

Commercial herbal supplements that have the word "standardized" on the label may seem to be the best choice. But standardization only means that the product has been tested to determine the type and amount of at least one active botanical constituent. While this can help improve the quality of encapsulated herbs, the method does have limitations. Research shows that the medicinal benefit of a particular herb does not necessarily reside in a particular constituent but rather comes from a complex combination of constituents. Standardization implies that only the standardized constituent is important. It's like labeling a carrot as containing a certain amount of beta-carotene, when carrots contain so many other healthful nutrients. Web sites such as www.consumerlab.com that base their entire assessment of a product on the presence of a standardized amount of a particular constituent do not give the whole picture. This is especially the case because some unethical companies try to beat the standardization system in various ways. That's why it's important to know that the company making the product and the company doing the testing are both legitimate and ethical.